peace○direct
WAR PREVENTION WORKS

peace direct is a growing movement of people determined to challenge violent responses to international, regional, national and local conflicts. We are committed to the peaceful resolution of conflict, and seek to support and promote the work of those who share these values.

We have three main aims:

1. Directly support those working in conflict areas to prevent atrocities and rebuild peace using nonviolent methods

At the front line of any conflict there are always people who would rather use nonviolent methods than pick up a weapon. Groups such as these in conflict areas need funds and resources, which are rarely available. **peace direct** aims to increase the resources and support available to people acting nonviolently. It identifies these people and puts them in touch with groups in the UK and worldwide. **peace direct** and these UK groups provide resources, offer solidarity and moral support, and engage in dialogue with governments regarding the policies that exacerbate conflicts. Groups in conflict areas show what can be done, building an understanding of the reality of the situation.

2. Raise the profile of nonviolent conflict resolution — to show how peaceful solutions can work, do work, and where they work

peace direct works towards transforming attitudes to war, challenging pessimism about alternatives to violence and reducing violence in conflict areas. It raises the public profile of conflict transformation so that conflict prevention and resolution become the main focus of charitable giving and government funding, and resources move away from military spending to nonviolent approaches.

3. Collect and publish evidence on the value and cost effectiveness of war prevention and conflict resolution in order to influence government policies and the allocation of public resources

peace direct supports and monitors peace-building activities, analyses the results and presents these to decision makers in the UK and elsewhere to develop a dialogue on destabilizing policies, e.g. the export of arms. We believe in respecting the knowledge and experience of those living and working nonviolently in conflict areas.

peace direct is a 'needs-led' organization, taking its cue from grass-roots experience, and making this comprehensible at policy level, for example to transfer budget allocations away from military equipment to human solutions to security problems. Our work builds on two decades of research into what works and what doesn't in terms of preventing, transforming and resolving conflict.

peaceOdirect

39a Lancaster Grove, London NW3 4HB
Tel: +44 (0)845 456 9714
Fax: +44 (0)20 7794 2489
www.peacedirect.org

UNARMED HEROES

THE COURAGE TO GO BEYOND VIOLENCE

*Personal testimonies and essays on
the peaceful resolution of conflict*

Compiled and edited by
peace direct

CLAIRVIEW

Clairview books
An imprint of Temple Lodge Publishing
Hillside House, The Square
Forest Row, RH18 5ES

www.clairviewbooks.com

Published by Clairview 2004

A catalogue record for this book is available from the British Library

ISBN 1 902636 52 X

Cover photographs of Caoimhe Butterly by Katie Barlow
Cover design by Andrew Morgan
Illustrations and typesetting by P.V. Vernon
Printed and bound by Cromwell Press Limited,
Trowbridge, Wilts.

Contents

You can do this too

Resources

Acknowledgements

There are many people we would like to thank from the bottom of our hearts. First, those who have told their stories in this book and have taken all the time and trouble necessary to do so. We appreciate their honesty and their boldness. A special thank you to Dr Elizabeth Winter who has been pivotal in reaching Dr Sima Samar.

Our gratitude goes to the volunteer editorial team: Deirdre O'Flinn who researched and interviewed contributors, a job she has done superbly and with sensitivity for their concerns; Rachael Burgess, who skilfully compiled the stories and was eventually persuaded to tell her own; Lorna Watson worked hard and long on the transcriptions with painstaking accuracy. Claire Devas, Cressida Langlands and Francesca Cerletti offered invaluable support from the **peace direct** office. We were delighted when Dina Glouberman agreed to contribute to the book; her wisdom gained from decades of helping people has proved invaluable to our efforts to make this a book the reader can really put to good use. We were so pleased that **peace direct**'s chair, Dame Anita Roddick, agreed to write the Foreword; she has shown in her own life and achievements how much personal courage can count at key moments.

A big thank you to P. V. Vernon, designer and typesetter, who has worked hard to please everyone. Lastly we would like to say how pleasant it has been to work with Sevak Gulbekian of Clairview Books, who understands what we are about, and has done everything possible to publish on schedule.

Foreword

by Dame Anita Roddick,
Founder, The Body Shop

What do ordinary people, people like you and me, do when faced with the reality of war? There are those of us who choose to fight — who think that war is an effective way to resolve conflict and who are prepared to risk our own lives, and to take the lives of others, in the name of our country or our God. At the other end of the scale there are those whose absolute condemnation of violent conflict leads them to seek peace, often through personal mediation between warring factions and mindless of their personal safety. And somewhere in between there is a huge raft of us ordinary people who are fed up with war being used to sort out disputes. But from the safety of our sitting-rooms we feel helpless to do anything about it.

It is the ordinary people who are acting courageously in the name of peace whose stories are in this book — people who have been thrown into situations of violence and conflict, or people dissatisfied with the direction the world seems to be taking, who decide peacefully to change 'their' world. This book is an emotional journey where you can feel the heart and soul of the protagonists being poured out onto the page. It's about anger, fear and hope, but mostly about reconciliation and the search for alternatives to violent and/or armed responses.

But this book is also about 'us', you and me: the readers. Remember 15 February 2003 and how impressive it was to see all those people marching against war. What energy there was. After such events we may feel powerless because those who make decisions seem not to listen to us. Even if confronted with violence and conflict we might still not know what to do because of our emotions — pain, fear or anger. How can we start to make a difference? *Unarmed Heroes* provides a reliable guide. It takes us through an emotional journey and enables us to think about ourselves, about what we value and believe in. It gives us the opportunity to gather our thoughts and start to take action.

This book spotlights the choices and struggles of those who choose the challenging path, the path of preventing killing, resolving conflict or simply influencing the policies that determine our lives. By telling the stories of those who made this choice, it also shows us how we can make a difference. I can see this book becoming one of the milestones in the creation of a strong, articulate and powerful peace constituency.

Introduction

by Dina Glouberman, PhD

This is an inspiring book and one that we greatly need today. It tells the story of people who, against the odds, have made a choice to heal and enrich the world, rather than meet violence with violence. Most of the people who tell their stories here have gone through incredibly painful experiences of the kind that could be expected to generate hate and revenge against those who have caused this pain. Yet they have chosen instead to devote their lives to peace and understanding, often at great cost to themselves.

For example:

Jo Berry's father was one of five people killed in the 1984 bombing by the IRA of the Conservative Party Conference in Brighton. After the initial shock, pain, rage and confusion, she could well have closed down her heart and mind to stop the terrible pain. She might even have gone on to live a life filled with that combination of powerlessness, rage and revenge that we can all feel when we consider ourselves to be victims of something someone else has done to harm us. Most of us would consider this to be a normal reaction.

This was the easy way, the obvious choice, and yet in the end it would have proved the difficult way because it has no resolution.

It is a path that winds its way through chronic resentment and hate, illness, breakdowns, poor relationships, and eventually a life not lived — a life that stopped one day and got stuck in one groove forever after.

Jo decided instead to go for understanding and deep healing — a path without a map whose destination is always home. She searched for a bigger picture, one which could help her to make a more complete sense of what had happened to her, whose truth could free her. To do so, she needed to tolerate an enormous amount of pain and confusion and to surrender all her old taken-for-granted ways of looking at things until she could find a new way forward.

Perhaps Jo's greatest challenge was her willingness to make friends with Patrick Magee, the IRA member who planted the bomb that killed her father. In so doing, she turned upside down everything she could have ever understood to be true about life. Most of us would find it hard even to conceive of taking this radical step.

Yet she tolerated this profound affront to what we would consider reason and normality and made it work for her and for all of us. Through her decision to take the difficult path, Jo not only came to some inner peace but was also able to commit herself to creating a more peaceful world in which such events do not happen.

Patrick Magee had a choice that was remarkably similar to Jo's. He could have continued to close down in much the same way as Jo. After all, he saw himself and his people as victims of an unjust social and political order. Although he may have been guilty of murder, he could have gone on believing that he was simply and correctly acting to right the wrongs of his people who themselves have been murdered and abused and discriminated against. He could well have resolved to continue killing until he and his people were listened to.

Instead, he too chose to step into a bigger picture. A crucial factor in this choice was his willingness to open himself up to dialogue with Jo Berry. To meet the daughter of the man who died as a result of the bomb you planted takes great courage. He must have known it would bring him great pain. He might not have known that it could ultimately help bring transformation.

Eventually Patrick left both the IRA and his old belief structures. He did not leave behind his most powerful ideals; he decided that the Republican cause could better be served by increased understanding between people from different sides of the fence. He set up and runs Causeway, which facilitates safe encounters between people who are victims and perpetrators of violence arising from the British/Irish conflict. In this he is supported by Jo. The two work together towards a more peaceful world.

Being inspiring

Stories like these can uplift us not so much because they are about extraordinary people doing extraordinary things, but rather because they are about ordinary people doing what human beings are capable of. We are inspiring when we transcend the situation we are thrust into by life to get a bigger picture of how things are and how things can be. We are inspiring when we go on to make a space in our lives to live out our part in that bigger picture. This is being human at its best.

Many of the people whose stories follow in this book have been thrust into a situation which involves a large dollop of world pain, the pain of being human in our present world. The particular form of world pain that they have been touched by is not the result of natural disasters, illness or emotional difficulties, but rather a direct expression of the social and political domain.

Some have been surrounded by conflict from childhood, perhaps in Northern Ireland, or in Israel, or in India. Others were catapulted into such a world by a difficult event, such as the death of a family member in a terrorist attack, or being rendered blind by a bomb. Others, less dramatically, always felt themselves to be alienated from a comfortable life in which the pain of the world was not satisfactorily addressed.

This book brings together strange companions. We have the stories here, as we have seen, by the daughter of a man killed by a bomb and the man who planted that bomb. We also have accounts by an Israeli Jew and by a Jerusalem-born Palestinian; by a former Loyalist terrorist and a former IRA terrorist; by members of the armed forces and by people who were victims of the armed forces. It is remarkable how similar are the deeper experiences of people who are normally viewed as diametrically opposed.

You could say that some have been victims and some have been perpetrators; clearly some had their lives shattered by bombs while others planted these bombs. And yet this language separates them from each other in ways none of them would accept now although they might once have done so.

In these days of a war against terrorism, people who plant bombs are often portrayed in the media as being less than human. Yet in these stories we can see the people who planted the bombs considered themselves to be victims of violence in their communities. Similarly, those who were victims of the bombs became obsessed at least for a while with revenge and violence. We are reminded that violence is often connected with a history of being a victim, and that being a victim often leads to thoughts if not acts of violence.

What makes these people stand out is the way they have dealt with their relationship to world pain. At some point, each one of them had a choice, the same seemingly easy way and seemingly difficult way that Jo and Patrick had. Again, the easy way can prove the most heartbreakingly difficult, and the difficult way can turn out to be the path to freedom and peace.

The difficult way always involves stepping into a bigger picture. How can we recognize the bigger picture? In the bigger picture, there can never be pure good on one side and pure bad on the other; it always includes everyone, and gives each person and each side a form of respect and empathy. The bigger picture requires us to live with all our complicated feelings no matter how painful they may be. The bigger picture asks us to act in such a way that the means are identical with the end; we cannot, for example, seek peace through violence or revenge. The bigger picture requires us to ditch all our old boxes and to step into the void in order to find our truth.

What do these unarmed heroes have in common?

Certain themes emerged for me when I read the stories of these ground-breaking peace workers:

- Often their first response to their pain was a desire to avenge the wrong. Eventually they began to see that nothing could be solved this way. The only way to take a step is to work towards a world in which such events didn't happen
- They chose to move away from seeing one side as right and one as wrong and strove to create a bigger understanding that included everyone
- They chose to surrender to the reality of all their feelings, and to be emotionally honest, no matter how much it hurt and confused them, without recourse to all their previous maps of right and wrong
- Those who had suffered the pain had to be willing to honour and understand those who had caused this pain, even if what they did was wrong. Those who had caused pain had to be willing to honour themselves, even if they now judged that what they did was wrong. Both had to trust themselves and each other to take this journey together
- There was usually no single turning-point, no lightning bolt that made everything clear. Transformation happened through a long, painful, tortuous process and had many turning-points and many periods of being stuck or even going backwards
- People generally moved from identifying with and caring for their family or their community to identifying with and caring for people all over the world in similar situations, including people who had been on the opposite side

- Often an opportunity to meet people who had been on the opposite side of the fence as well as facilitators to help them with their feelings and attitudes made the process easier
- There was a price to pay, not only in terms of their own process but because it meant a separation from their old community and old belief systems
- What they got in return was a bigger world community, a more universal belief system, and an opportunity to be of service.

What can you learn from these stories?

I found these stories difficult to read. They are not written in a single voice, for example, or by professional writers. But that is their beauty. They are real, they are front-line accounts from people whose styles are very different from each other, written in the ways that the individuals preferred, some by interview, some gleaned from source material, some written directly by the person. Some accounts focus more on being and becoming, while others are more concerned with doing and acting. None are written with the 'moral of the story' spelled out.

Each of the conflicts in these stories has links to our lives. We may be reminded of conversations we have with our friends and family about the Middle East, or about how our favourite newspaper covers the global war on terror. We may think about for whom we vote and how we keep them accountable, or consider how all of this global tension is reflected in our local communities whether it be on issues relating to the asylum seekers, British National Party, abused women or whatever.

We might still be tempted to see the accounts of these 'unarmed heroes' as the stories of others rather than as an inspiration to find a new story for ourselves. Yet it is urgent that we put ourselves into the picture. This is not only because the world need is very pressing, but also because our need to be of service is pressing.

To be of service is both an inner commitment and an outer one. Some of us will be more inclined to work on reaching an inner resolution through psychotherapy or prayer or other forms of personal and spiritual development. Others will be inclined to reach for an outer resolution by political and social action that seeks to guarantee that this will never happen again. Both these responses are valid and powerful. However we can no longer afford to choose one at the expense of the other.

If we go for a personal and spiritual solution for ourselves alone, we will lose out on a feeling of connection and contribution. All great teachers and gurus have shown that it is not possible to achieve real peace or real enlightenment by cutting off from our community. There is a natural generosity within all of us that makes us feel that we do not want others to suffer what we have suffered. If we don't honour this we will feel ultimately unfulfilled or worse. This doesn't, by the way, mean we have to 'do' something in the conventional sense of 'doing'. Some people are natural supporters, teachers and catalysts by simply being who they are as fully as possible. This is not about standing by and taking the easy way out, but about finding the way we can each contribute.

On the other hand, if we choose social and political action alone, we can despite our good intentions create further strife around us through the feelings we have disowned. Whatever we do not understand and live with in ourselves may be projected outwards onto the world and lead to hurt, misunderstanding and battle. We all know that with the best ideals in the world we can end up seeing our friends as enemies and our enemies as evil or subhuman. This is not going to create a more peaceful world.

We also know that we can end up feeling exhausted, disillusioned and angry. In my work with people who have burnt out, it becomes clear that doing a good and inspiring job is not enough, as many devoted workers have found to their cost. Any of us could burn out if we look around at everything that needs doing in the world, decide to devote our lives to it in an effort to right the wrongs of this world and then work harder and harder to accomplish what is essentially an impossible task.

We might well slowly become more and more tired and disheartened, more and more empty or cynical or chronically angry, more and more prone to illness. We would be likely eventually to become less and less effective. We might even get to the stage where we collapse and can do nothing at all.

If we look more deeply, we may find that some of the motivation for this work comes from an unresolved need to rescue others from the pain that we find too hard to bear. When we operate from this place, we often get deeply disappointed and disillusioned when things do not work out as we wish.

The key is to find work that our heart and mind and soul support us to do, and then to do it without asking for results. In order to do this, we need to go through a process that is less like looking around for what needs doing and more like sensing where the energy between us and the world calls us to go. It is what I call 'listening to the whispering of our soul'. Some of the questions and imagery exercises in this book are designed to help us do that.

Peace and generosity

In my view, doing both the inner and the outer work is the greatest challenge of our lives and of our times. We need to express our search to reach peace through facing the complicated truths of our inner life, and we also need to express that natural generosity that asks us to offer the fruits of our learning to an aching world.

The people who tell their story here can help to teach us not so much how to do it, but that it can be done — even in the most difficult and heartbreaking circumstances. Their simplicity and modesty hits us with the deep knowledge that if they can do it so can we. And if we can do it, so can others we meet. We can all bear witness that to be human is to be inspired and inspiring.

THE STORIES

Jo Berry

Jo has been on a long journey of healing since her father, Sir Anthony Berry MP, was killed in the IRA bombing of the 1984 Tory Party Conference in Brighton. Her passion is to help stop the cycle of violence and revenge. This has led her to many experiences in N. Ireland since her first visit in 1985. She eventually met Patrick Magee, who was convicted of the Brighton bombing, in November 2000. Their meeting led to a BBC documentary broadcast in December 2001, and

subsequent interviews and broadcasts together. Jo is part of the Legacy Project *based at the Warrington Peace Centre. She is preparing to train as an emotional facilitator as she sees a need for creating safe places in which both victims and victimizers can share their stories.*

My father, Sir Anthony Berry MP, was killed when an IRA bomb blew up the Grand Hotel in Brighton during the 1984 Conservative Party Conference. I had never considered that dad was a target for the IRA and it came as a huge shock, ripping my heart in two and changing the very essence of who I was. I had to tell my younger siblings that their dad was dead and mum injured. I could no longer travel freely around the world without care or responsibility. I felt that I had been catapulted into a war about which I knew nothing, but which now became my war. Now I cared passionately; I felt the pain of the families of everyone killed by the bomb and wanted to somehow bring something positive out of the tragedy. I knew that I had a choice in the days after the bomb: to stay as a victim, blaming others for my pain, or to go on a journey of healing in search of understanding. I wanted to understand why my dad had been killed. I made an inner commitment to the journey with no idea what that meant, but I knew that life would give me the experiences I needed to learn.

During the first year I began to walk in the footsteps of the bomber. By chance I met the brother of an IRA man who had been killed by the British Army. We looked beyond the label of 'enemy' and talked of our shared humanity and dreams for a peaceful world. Together we built a bridge across the political divide. I corresponded with a Republican prisoner who shared his story with me, and I spent an afternoon with a politician from Sinn Fein. I began to understand the conditions of injustice and oppression that had led to the bombing. In my world people I loved could be blown up and I felt a deep sense of responsibility to help bring about peace. This gave me a sense of purpose and a belief that I could contribute to the peace process by helping to build bridges through meeting so-called enemies as human beings.

During 1986 I was part of a TV programme on forgiveness, after which I felt I could go no further. I left London for North Wales, married and had three daughters. I call this time 'crying in the desert'. I felt so involved with N. Ireland, crying with every bomb and death, yet unable to find a way to go there. I was in deep shock and was offered no help. I know now that I locked some of the trauma away to deal with when I was ready.

Thirteen years later, in August 1999, Patrick Magee, the IRA man who had been convicted of planting the bomb, was released from prison under the Good Friday Agreement. I relived the day of my dad's death as if for the first time. I felt the grief and shock again, and had a deep rage at Magee. 'How dare he kill my dad? How dare he destroy my family?' I cried and screamed, my arms beating up and down in anger and rage. I knew this was the time to become involved with my journey again.

Through a couple of synchronicities I found myself in a victims' support group at Glencree Centre for Reconciliation in the Wicklow Mountains. I met victims from all sides of the conflict including ex-prisoners who knew Pat Magee; this was important preparation for me. I dived into my feelings and felt so much grief, anger and sadness. I knew that it was safe to share my story as no one would be afraid of my pain and I found it to be a great deal of comfort and joy in connecting with other victims.

After the first meeting of ex-prisoners I experienced feelings of betrayal. I felt that I was betraying my family, my country and other victims of terrorism. These feelings were overwhelming. When I processed them I cried for hours and found that lying underneath were feelings of deep sadness. By meeting the so-called enemies I had discovered to my surprise how likeable and normal they were. Did this mean that my dad needn't have died? Emotionally I had discovered the waste of war, and realized that the 'enemy' is always my brother and sister. Through healing the trauma in me I was finding my voice and learning to trust myself more. I had longed to build a bridge with Patrick, my motivation being to meet him as a human being and to hear his story. On 24 November 2000 I met Patrick Magee for the first time. I was terrified that he wouldn't turn up but he did. He was very open and told me, 'I want to hear your anger, I want to hear your pain.'

We talked for three hours with an intensity I had not experienced before. It was a profoundly healing experience that left me feeling elated and yet disorientated. On a deep level I felt as if I already knew him. I felt disorientated because I felt as if I'd broken one of society's taboos by meeting Pat. I remember walking down the street and wondering what others would think if they knew what I'd done. My world felt topsy-turvy; it was as if I was climbing a mountain without a map, and I felt out of my depth and alone again. However it soon became clear that Pat was willing to go on a journey with me. I met him with my heart open and took responsibility for my feelings. We met on many occasions, often on our own for several hours at a time. We agreed that some of our meetings could be filmed for a BBC2 *Everyman* documentary called *Facing the Enemy*, which was screened in December 2001.

The cost for me has been in leaving my emotional comfort zone and entering new territories where the old rules no longer apply. I have been challenged on every level through meeting Pat and going public with the documentary. The only way for me to get through this is with emotional honesty, feeling every feeling without judging it or trying to change it. I have experienced shock, grief and pain on a deep level, because since the bomb my life has been changed forever and I have had to grieve about the loss that involved in order to move on. I've questioned whether I've put too much strain on my marriage and whether it's fair on my children. I've been taken to the edge through having an emotional pattern of doubting myself. I've found myself grieving for the me that died at the time of the bomb. I've feared that I've made the worst mistake of my life. I've been terrified that I'm not up to the exposure and also of my vulnerability being seen in public. I've had feelings of betrayal about hurting and re-traumatizing other victims. I've felt angry with Pat because even now he still intellectually defends the bombing.

I'm uneasy with the word 'forgiveness' as I feel that if I forgive Patrick I will never again be able to feel challenging emotions such as rage and anger. And yet, I've had an experience of such empathy with him that I've felt there is nothing to forgive. I have walked in Patrick's footsteps for a long time and a part of me has finally reached a place of understanding and acceptance. This is strengthened by discovering his humanity as I get to know him. The judgements fall away as I realize that if I had lived his life I may have made the same decisions. This experience stays with me and gives me the freedom to feel all of my emotions. It is a hugely demanding process, but by knowing that I am in charge of my experience I've learnt to look after myself emotionally.

Meeting Pat has given me so many opportunities for healing and transformation. And I've learnt that the only betrayal is that of my heart. My heart, that can encompass all my feelings, tells me to keep opening to transform all the pain, grief and fear into compassion. I am beginning to heal the parts of me that blame and dehumanize others when I'm hurting. My compassion is growing as I accept that Pat is now a friend and an important person in my life, although it is still very challenging to parts of me that I call Pat my friend. It's now two years since we met and we are still in close contact. As our care for one another grows we become more vulnerable, and our working together becomes even harder.

But however fragile and scared I may feel, I've seen that our experience resonates with others and this strengthens my commitment to the work that we're doing. In learning to trust myself I have found there is a place deep inside me that keeps me going when I want to give up. Sharing our story at conferences and at victim/perpetrator support groups is very challenging for us both; we never know what's going to come up and how we are going to feel at the time. Nevertheless, we are committed to continue working together for peace and reconciliation and my sense is that this is only the beginning of our journey.

I could not have travelled so far without my family, my old and new friends holding my hand as I walked and sometimes stumbled. Although I never had structured support I have been blessed by meeting many inspiring and loving people who have given me so much during times of need. Looking back I can see that Pat and I met in the most challenging way as there was no facilitation or ongoing support available. I am involved in the Causeway project with Pat in which research is being done into how to create safe spaces so that similar meetings to ours can be conducted in a more healing way. Everyone involved in the N. Ireland conflict needs opportunities to be heard, healed and supported. My experience has also led me to train as an emotional facilitator and furthermore be involved with the Legacy Project in Warrington.

I had become so close to my dad during that summer before he was killed. We had moved from being father and daughter to becoming good friends who supported each other and understood our differences; we had very different lifestyles but we shared a vision of peace. Now, I am left with a deep gratitude that I have an opportunity to work for peace and to end the cycle of violence and revenge. I know the importance of looking at the complex roots of violence and to understand that from the deepest individual level right through to whole communities we are all responsible for creating the conditions that support violence as a way of meeting needs. It is so easy to blame, to project our violence onto others. I feel connected to those around the world who are saying no to the cycle of violence, and knowing about them gives me strength. The miracle was that Patrick was prepared to go on a journey with me and could regard it as something that was helping him. He said that the personal cost of his violence was having lost some of his humanity; and now, having me in his life he is able to find it again. He sees my dad as a real person rather than as a faceless enemy. I see the way forward is to recognize and experience the humanity in our enemy as our own. I believe that everyone deserves opportunities to have their humanity restored, and to that end my passion to work for peace and reconciliation continues to grow.

Patrick Magee

Patrick was born in Belfast in 1951, grew up in Norwich, and returned to Ireland in 1971. As a former IRA (Irish Republican Army) volunteer, he spent a total of 17 years in prison. In 1985 he was sentenced to eight life sentences for his role in the Brighton bomb. Shortly after his release under licence in 1999 under the terms of the Good Friday Agreement, he gained a doctorate from the University of Ulster, Coleraine. An emended version of his thesis was published in 2001: Gangsters or

Guerrillas: Representations of Irish Republicans in 'Troubles Fiction' (Beyond the Pale, Belfast, ISBN 1-900960-14-1). Patrick and Jo Berry, daughter of Sir Anthony Berry, who was killed in the Brighton bomb, collaborated on the BBC2 documentary, Facing the Enemy, *broadcast in December 2001, and he is now in the process of establishing Causeway, a project to facilitate safe encounters between victims and perpetrators of actions arising from the British / Irish conflict.*

I was born in Belfast in 1951, but when I was four, my father brought us over to England. He had served an apprenticeship in the shipyards, but at the end of the apprenticeship, there was no job there. My father always attributed that to bigotry on the shop floor because he was a Catholic and it was a preserve of Protestants. However, he managed to find work in Norwich and got a house for us there.

My father was always very opposed to bigotry, and that came from his experience in Belfast because I think he would have liked to have stayed in Ireland. That intolerance of prejudice is perhaps his greatest gift to me.

If we go back a generation, relatives on both sides of the family were active Republicans. For example, my grandfather, Joss Magee, had been imprisoned in Crumlin Road Prison and on the internment ship *Argenta* in the twenties because of his involvement. And two of my mother's uncles had also been held on the *Argenta*, but that background never really featured in conversations. I was aware of it, but it wasn't a big thing. I was certainly under no pressure to think along those lines. But when things really started to unfold in Belfast, I was naturally drawn to understand more. I felt very alienated — I didn't feel part of English life — and I used to contrast that with the welcome of Belfast, and the affinity with relatives who used to come and visit us from Belfast. There was a natural identification with Belfast and I always thought of it as 'home' despite growing up in Norwich.

In late 1970, I took a trip back to Ireland. There was a lot of civil strife, riots and so forth, and I was a witness to some of that and took my impressions back to England with me. The turning-point for me was the introduction of internment without trial in August 1971. I was working in Blackpool at the time and I decided to return to Belfast. I remember walking up the Falls Road to an aunt's house, a journey of some four miles. It was a Sunday morning and there were no buses except the burnt out buses at the side of the road. I had a big cardboard suitcase full of clothes. I saw milling crowds on the street corners, and there was debris from the previous night's rioting and the smell of gunpowder. It was incredible. I walked all the way up there with this suitcase and nobody was paying me any attention at all. So that was my introduction. I didn't come back to join the conflict, but I did come back to understand the situation. I wanted to contribute something, but I didn't know what I could do. I ended up living in a place called Unity Flats — my father had lived there before marrying my mother — and it was a real flashpoint, a small Catholic enclave facing onto a larger Protestant area so there was constant trouble. There was no one single event that caused me to join the Republican movement — it was an accumulation of things. It is hard to explain motivations, they are always complex, but I was struck by the way Republicans were organized to look after people's welfare needs. In this Catholic enclave, like other nationalist areas throughout the six counties, people had just been written off and there was no outside agency providing for them. If they didn't look after themselves, no one was going to do it for them. The outside world had to be made aware of this injustice and so nationalists took to the streets to make those in power listen. There was a feeling that this, the civil rights campaign, was the right course. The outcome was that we were driven off the streets — clamped down on and contained — and as a result many people, including myself, joined the IRA.

Looking back, I realize that our response was a consequence of our own history. We had never had the strength sufficient to counter the injustices facing us or to resolve our grievances. No one was going to give us that strength, no one was going to empower us, so we had to do it ourselves. It was a long, costly, drawn out business.

As a result of my activities in the early seventies, I ended up being interned and got out at the tail end of 1975. While I was in prison, I did a lot of thinking about what I was going to do upon release, and it struck me very clearly that if we were going to be listened to we had to do something more drastic. The British strategy was 'containment'. The British establishment would have been happy to settle for decades of bombs in Belfast, so if bombs were to make a difference they had to be targeted at the establishment outside Belfast. I came out of internment in 1975 with a very clear idea of what I was going to do. I wasn't able to do it immediately, but eventually I did end up on active service across the water. I didn't see any other way to reverse British policy. It was a natural progression.

In 1981, as a consequence of the hunger strike and the election of Bobby Sands in a failed attempt to change Thatcher's stance, we woke up as a movement, and not just the leadership, to the need to enter electoral politics and to harness that strength to further our objectives. Traditionally, Republicans were deeply suspicious of the electoral process. They were sick of the system and wanted to smash it. But suddenly, in order to save the hunger strikers, there was an agreement to stand for elections. Because of the hunger strikers, there was a constituency of support that had faith in us and I quickly recognized that this had to be the way forward. So prior to the hunger strike I would have been opposed to that course, but in its aftermath I had changed. The momentum was behind us and we couldn't be contained. The more we grew in strength, the more the realization grew that this was the way forward. We were approaching the position where we had sufficient strength to say: there is now the potential of a viable alternative to armed struggle. Much still had to be done, but that year was the watershed.

Unfortunately, the political establishment was hell bent on a military solution in spite of the advice of its own generals who clearly stated that the IRA could not be defeated. You would think that this would have occasioned a rethink, but unfortunately, in 1979, Margaret Thatcher was in government. It was well trumpeted that Airey Neave was her choice to be the Secretary of State for Northern Ireland, and that he would pursue a very hard line, so it was just a wasted opportunity. There was a dearth of political vision and foresight.

There are certain things I can't talk about — operational matters — but I do stand by my involvement as an IRA volunteer, including the Brighton operation. Its aim was to enable the Republican movement to demonstrate its commitment to the long haul, that as long as Britain remained in Ireland they would meet resistance, that we would not be contained and that the struggle would not be confined to the six counties.

I should explain what it means to me to be a Republican. In the context of the conflict, for me, Republican aims are best expressed by Tom Paine. Paine wasn't talking about a particular form of government, but what government was for: to represent the people — not a majority, nor an elite, but all the people or, I should say, all their legitimate interests (provided of course that these didn't cut across the legitimate interests of others). And that at heart is all Republicans are trying to achieve. You ask Republicans what they are struggling for and they'll say 'a united Ireland, the end of partition', but this is the means to an end. Unification of the country merely provides a means to attain that wider Republican goal of a fully inclusive democracy. What the struggle is really about is the fight for rights.

Now I personally think I can do more to further Republican ends outside of the movement than inside, but I would still call myself a Republican. I have respect for the Unionist position to the extent that it's based on cultural, social and historic links. But I don't subscribe to the idea that the six counties are reformable or that the equality agenda can be furthered purely in the context of the six counties. That is why the Good Friday Agreement is the baseline, because it recognizes all the political dimensions, the north/south and the east/west dimensions.

Republicans have been criticised for their recourse to violent methods. I am a lapsed Catholic, but I have been sustained throughout my involvement in the conflict by the belief that my actions had a moral basis. Looking back, I don't think we had a choice. There were genuine grievances — disparities in welfare and the allocation of resources — and these fuelled the conflict. After 50 years of misrule — Unionist misrule but the buck stopped at Westminster — people felt the state had abandoned them so a political solution wasn't open to us. In the end, I was impelled by my experiences on the streets of Belfast, by the things I had witnessed. That's where my commitment to Republicanism comes from.

An important turning-point in my life was my meeting with Jo Berry on 24 November 2000. I met her first in Dublin for three hours. I can't remember now much of the detail of what we talked about but we both felt that something very significant had happened. The Brighton bombing had suddenly plummeted her into this conflict, and she wanted to put her loss, her father's death, into some kind of context. She wanted to understand — I suppose in some sense to get closure. She hasn't attained it yet. But I think she has been strengthened by these meetings. I certainly have, because it has occasioned me to look back over the past and to deal with some of the difficult issues — the fact that I hurt human beings, the fact that I hurt Jo.

A tangible result of these meetings was the establishment of Causeway, which aims to facilitate similar encounters between victims and former combatants, a project warmly endorsed by Jo.

We aim to be totally inclusive — non-sectarian, non-partisan and cross-community. The membership of the management board reflects all the different constituencies. The goal isn't so much restitution but understanding. I think that's an attainable and necessary goal. And you do that by extensive preparation before you bring people together. So you'd be asking questions like, 'What are you willing to discuss?' 'What is the agenda?' and perhaps more important, 'What don't you want to discuss?' For example, Republicans would be obviously reluctant to talk about operational matters. But there's much that can be explored — so it's finding that out and setting an agenda. It's also important to have the right environment. The danger is that you could actually re-traumatize people so you have to create a space that is psychologically safe. It isn't easy. Jo is a remarkable woman — she came a long way on her journey on her own in isolation and she has actually become a friend. When people come together, they are no longer faceless victims or enemies. Now, when I talk to Jo, incredible as this may sound, it is as if we are sitting and discussing the hurt I have caused to a friend. That's the big change. It doesn't get any easier because of that. So an awful lot of thinking has to be ploughed into bringing people together. That is what Causeway is about.

We're at an early stage and are only now embarking on seeking the needed funding to develop the project. I would expect a limited take-up initially, but the need is there and, given all we have come through, will be there for perhaps decades. For example, when I talk to Republicans about this, some of them argue that this is premature because the conflict isn't yet resolved. But I think you need to prepare the ground for conflict resolution with initiatives like this. Much has been lost. There are many dimensions to that loss. I have a son who was seven at the time of my capture in 1985 and I've had little contact with him because of my incarceration in England. He is a victim. And that truth extends into practically every home in the North. We are only beginning to recognize the extent of problems needing to be tackled if we are to leave the past behind.

A lot of people talk about the truth and reconciliation format, but you're never going to get that here. In South Africa, you had a government, a sovereign power, prepared to accept its culpability and admit that apartheid was wrong. I can't envisage a day when the British Government will fully acknowledge or accept its culpability. They had choices, but they refused them and instead resorted to repression and containment of the struggle to prevent people from getting their rights. No one side is blameless. Republicans repudiate this hierarchy of culpability that excludes the role of Britain in the political mess, which as the sovereign power it created.

You can point the finger of blame at them, but the total absence of any sense of culpability means that there's not going to be a comprehensive, meaningful truth and reconciliation process here — meaningful in the sense of addressing our collective trauma and in doing so putting a line under the past and moving on together. But that doesn't mean you do nothing now. We have to address our own culpability, and all constituencies should be involved.

Martin Snoddon

Released from prison on licence in 1990 after 15 years as a political prisoner in Long Kesh prison camp, Martin has consistently worked on a number of projects focusing on alleviating causes for conflict and addressing the legacy of the violent conflict in and about Northern Ireland. He is currently the Centre Director of the Multi-Agency Resource Centre and sits as a member of both the Board of Trustees of the Mediation Network and the Board of Trustees of the Healing Through

Remembering Project. Previously, Martin founded and developed the Ex-Prisoners Interpretative Centre (EPIC), a reintegration programme for Loyalist Political ex-prisoners, and was instrumental in the development of the Greater Shankill Alternatives Restorative Justice Programme.

My story began even before I was born. I inherited the conflict that had been erupting periodically in N. Ireland ever since 1922. It was in the sixties when I was a teenage boy that the conflict was visited on me in the area where I lived. But, apart from the violence, I have to say that I often look back on my early childhood days and smile because they were so enjoyable — kicking a ball against the wall for hours on end, climbing trees, going over boulders in the rivers, all those childhood things. It was tremendous and I remember the innocence that was in my mind at the time. Of course, like most other children in Belfast then, come Sunday, I was ordered to go to Sunday school. So I was aware of Christianity and its moral teaching, aware of the difference between right and wrong. More than that, I would say that those values were internalized. I had seen my parents practise them — and actions do speak louder than words. As a result of this upbringing there were many occasions when I helped other people, and it was probably through that impulse to help other people that I engaged in the conflict when it came to my neighbourhood.

It's important to make clear that when conflict came to my neighbourhood it came as oppression from the IRA (Irish Republican Army). About 500 of my co-religionist neighbours were put out of their homes. There were bomb explosions and shootings almost on a daily basis. So my first introduction to the violent conflict was in defence of my neighbours — in the absence of adequate state protection for its citizens. The state security forces were obviously very stretched at the time (1970 we're talking about here). The British army had just arrived. My particular neighbourhood was a small Protestant community in the vastly larger nationalist community of West Belfast. What was happening was that Protestants were being put out of their homes, and I often found myself as a teenager helping to carry out the furniture. I remember going to the top of Lanadane Avenue carrying a Union Jack with me. (The British army were trying to segregate us at that time and were moving two old people out of their homes). The British army came rushing up afterwards in their Land-Rovers. But they hadn't come to help the old people — they had come to look for the Union flag — which I had safely tucked up under my jacket. I carried the television out on to the lorry as they were searching for the flag. This was typical of many occasions when no sooner had Protestants been evacuated from their homes than a Catholic family was moved in.

In 1972, the IRA ceasefire broke down in Lanadane Avenue. This was the street that I had played in as a child; where my school friends had grown up was an onslaught of the IRA shooting down on us — I think it was for about eleven days. I was dodging the bullets as I roamed the street. This was common you know, nothing extraordinary. I was just one of the people trying to help people in those circumstances. But I found myself, a 16-year-old, having a gun put in my hand. The violence wasn't forced on me, but neither was it welcomed. I would say that I was a very reluctant combatant but I did feel it necessary to defend my community, my friends and family and people that I loved and who were in danger. How I chose to do that was to take up arms against those aggressors. So I was tending to terrorize terrorists. That was my aim and my motivation.

At the age of 19, I found myself in the Belfast criminal court to receive a life sentence for causing an explosion. We had been attacking an IRA base in North Belfast. It was fortified with wire grilles and wire grates and there were meant to be two armed security guards, but there weren't any when we got there. As we started our attack, the bomb exploded prematurely within two feet of me. My colleague who was standing shoulder to shoulder with me died six weeks later from that explosion. A woman died on the premises and 17 people were injured. I picked myself up from the rubble and could hardly see for smoke and dust. I could smell burned flesh and my clothes were blown off me and I had burns and various injuries. I made my way up the street and was caught in Belfast Lock by a crowd from the Nationalist side. I had tried to head under a railway bridge. It was dark and I heard them shouting, 'There's the bastard.' I could feel the flames on my back and that's why I was heading towards the lock to extinguish them. I had very few clothes on the bottom half of my body, because the front of my jeans had been blown away. They caught me in the lock and they beat me up. Then they tried to drag me from the lock to the bridge to hang me there. At that point, the British military police came on the scene and took me off the crowd. They proceeded to beat me, smashing my head in the process.

Then the RUC (Royal Ulster Constabulary) arrived and they took me to the police station where they too started to beat me, but by that time I wasn't feeling the blows any more. The police doctor came in and ordered them to take me immediately to the Belfast Royal Victoria Hospital. On the way to the operating theatre they were still asking me questions but I refused to answer.

I remember waking the next morning after the operation and seeing the effect of the bomb explosion, and the fact that a woman had died in that explosion tore the heart clean out of me. If 120 men had died I would have felt better. Our intelligence at the time was that this was an active base and this has since been confirmed by members of the IRA. Even so, the fact that a woman was killed ate into my conscience for a long time.

I received a life sentence and found myself in Long Kesh prison. It was a front line of sorts with several different organizations at war with each other sharing the same space. It was also like a prisoner of war camp — you had your Nissen huts, watch-towers, dogs, barbed wire and so on. We lived in a regimental style and maintained military discipline with parades, duties and study. I was the leader of the UVF (Ulster Volunteer Force) and became second in command of all the Loyalist cadres. I took part in a lot of drilling, and also drilled other people. The authorities viewed me as a hardliner and I really was a hardliner in the sense that I was not going to allow them to criminalize me. The authorities were carrying out a review and I refused to participate because I saw this as an attempt at criminalization. Consequently, I was not viewed too kindly by the authorities and they tried to knock me back time and time again. Nevertheless, I took part in a university degree programme and in 1986, along with four other UVF prisoners, I received an honours degree while I was still in Long Kesh. We were the first political prisoners to get degrees.

The formal education I received was of great value to me, but the informal education was more life changing. I said that Long Kesh was a front line of sorts, but it was also a 'back channel' of sorts since it provided opportunities for informal contacts between former enemies. We had a lot of discussions amongst ourselves, but we also had discussions with members of the official IRA. I remember one member in particular who studied alongside me. I remember the first day we met. There was some hesitation over making the tea — was he going to spit in it or was I? But I'm proud to say that we became very close friends and studied together for a number of years. After he was released, he came up to visit me, which was mind-boggling for the prison officers at the time. Also, some of my comrades then wouldn't have appreciated the friendship.

During the course of my imprisonment, I had a lot of time for self-examination. There wasn't any immediate transformation; there was no light that came on in my cell to tell me there was forgiveness. I'm afraid it wasn't that easy. In fact it was tortuous. There were a lot of beliefs and attitudes that I had held dear that I was breaking down and building up anew while I was in prison. A lot of people were going though the same process. We explored the motivations for the conflict, not just the immediate effects, and examined Irish history in detail — the pros and cons, the different stories, the propaganda and the political attitudes involved in Irish history.

By the time I got my life licence I had served 15 years, and so in 1990 I was back on the streets of Belfast. I remember soaking up that sense of freedom at Mary Peters track — the colour of green as opposed to the drab greyness of the prison. It was tremendous. It just seeped through my body, the silence of the early morning — it's a memory that's still very much alive in me.

There had been structural changes in Belfast that were due to the combatants, but probably most striking was that views that had been extremist before I went to prison had become very much the middle ground. And I was meant to reintegrate into this society that was tearing itself to pieces. That was not the society I wanted to live in. I wanted to change it so that other people would not have to go through the experience of violence that I had had. By 1992 I was in a relationship and in August I had a son. This gave an impetus to my need to bring about change — the need to bring peace and a reconciliation of these polarized views.

During 199–91, I participated in a group concerned with the reintegration of political prisoners from both sides. There were representatives of the Provisional IRA — actually nine of them — and three of us from the UVF. There were also several social activists. The meeting was chaired by a Quaker, a man called Barney Rafferty, who had worked in the prisons — a man I hold in highest esteem. We had many meetings and discussions about the problems, and the group became known as PROPP — Progressive Release of Political Prisoners. It wasn't just release from the confines of prison; it was release from the emotional turmoil associated with reintegration. We dealt with the practical problems as well — housing, welfare and so forth. At first, there was a lack of trust. We were all vulnerable because the conflict was still going on. It would have been very easy for someone to talk, and any one of us could be targeted, or indeed, have targeted someone else. So trust had to be built up, and in the end it was built up and agreements were kept.

At the same time, I was trying to re-establish myself in normal society. I had a job as a computer training coordinator at the cross-community Boundary organization in the city centre. There I trained quite a number of people in computer skills to the NVQ level. We had a complete suite with state of the art computer stations, which was quite an achievement if you knew where the organization had been before I started there. We had secured £120,000 from a funder for two centres, one based in nationalist West Belfast and the other in loyalist East Belfast. Those areas had been targeted because there was a predominance of ex-prisoners in those areas.

In 1995, I gave up my full-time post and the security that went with it and started as a coordinator of the Loyalist ex-prisoners interpretive centre on a six-month contract — quite foolish most people would think, including myself sometimes. However, there was a driving force which I feel they understood — there was some 'game' that directed me at the time. Very soon after I started, a special programme for peace and reconciliation was introduced, financed by the European fund, and with those financial resources I was able to further develop the centre — add staff and create different satellite bases round the province. I was contributing in many other ways towards peace. A lot of that was concerned with dialogue for understanding, to help other people understand.

During this time, a lot of boundaries were pushed back. There were formal meetings in which Loyalists and Republicans shared platforms and participated in various events. There were attempts to address the legacy of conflict in the local community. For example, many young people were engaging in substance abuse and we helped them by making our premises available. Punishment attacks also continued, and I was instrumental in developing a programme to deal with this problem based on the philosophy of restorative justice (for a while I was chair of its management committee). This is a very effective process and it is still operating today.

I was fortunate during those five years between 1995 and 2000 to have received various forms of training, from trauma counselling to mediation and negotiation skills. But I couldn't have attempted this work if I hadn't become reconciled with my own past. I have seen others stumble in their attempts at reconciliation because there were unresolved conflicts in their own minds. Reconciliation with my past came about while I was still in prison. A lot of it was about understanding and accepting my motives for becoming involved in violence. At the root of it all, I believe that I acted with good intentions on behalf of my community in the face of the threat that existed at that time. At the same time, I fully appreciated the impact of my actions on other people — the families of those killed, the woman who was blown up, my comrades and other people who were on the premises. My family was very law abiding and they did not support my actions, but they stood by me as their son, partly perhaps because they were witnessing the events themselves and the bellicose rhetoric from politicians and the media. Nevertheless, I came to believe that what I did was wrong — absolutely morally wrong.

Now, in the work I am doing, there are several sources of strength that keep me going. The future of my son is a strong incentive for me. There is also the fact that I have participated in violence and understand its human cost. But there is also a spiritual dimension. I am not a religious person, but things that have occurred in the course of my life — my survival after the explosion, the attacks of the crowd which should have killed me, and other events like people coming into my life at just the right time and bringing skills and knowledge — all these things make me feel that there is some kind of divine intervention in my life.

There have been some costs to me in doing this work. A lot of my former comrades would not agree with some or all of my actions and a lot of friendships have broken down as a result. There has been an emotional cost in knowing that they think I have distanced myself from my community, when in fact I now have a much wider sense of community than the purely parochial one. And that wider sense of community includes people who were my enemies and supporters of my former enemies. This sense of a wider community has been reinforced by visits to other areas of conflict. I've been to South Africa and have seen the poverty and deprivation in the townships. I explored some of the history of that conflict and have felt a great deal of compassion for them in the circumstances that they faced. They were part of my awakening. I've visited Nicaragua and spoken with Contras and Sandanistas, people who were also killing each other at one point. And when I shared their suffering and tried to address their needs and their communities' needs, I found it a source of strength that there were like-minded people in the world even though it was a different conflict context.

At a conference in Nicaragua, I spoke with people from Guatemala, Columbia, Mozambique and Angola. It was the fourth international conference of ex-combatants and peace builders. There were two of us from the Northern Hemisphere — one former member of the Provisional IRA and myself. We shared a lot of our personal stories and became very good trusting friends as a result. We still have our separate and polarized political aspirations, but one thing that I have ingrained within me is an acceptance of difference regardless of what that difference is. There is one point though on which I am implacable and that is that I am opposed to the use of violence. I can't say I'm a pacifist since if someone attacked my son and only violence could stop him, then I would act violently to prevent that hurt. But I'm opposed to the use of violence to achieve social or political ends.

At a more personal level there have been some costs to me in doing this work. Three years ago, I was emotionally exhausted and absolutely drained and overwhelmed by people's pain and suffering to the point that I was a physical wreck and had to be put on medication. I couldn't even watch television or listen to the radio. So I had to take time out. I've had to learn that lesson painfully that I need to wring out some of the pain that I hear from others on a daily basis. I've had to find ways of releasing myself and to discipline myself to take breaks. Prior to that, I would work into the early hours of the morning. Now I find I'm forcing myself to watch the most ridiculous TV programmes you can imagine just to have a break. I have to practise what I preach. If we don't take care of ourselves, we are less use to other people.

People often ask me why I became so involved in peace work. I can only say I became involved because of compassion for my community. I have been out of prison for twelve years now and have been involved in peace building all that time. I look around me and see that most people in N. Ireland are not involved. They weren't involved in the violence as I was, and so they have less reason to be involved in building peace. You could say that the very motive of compassion that first drove me into violence later drove me into peacemaking.

Anat Levy Reisman

Anat is a women's mediator and trainer based in Israel. She believes that the option of sitting on the fence does not exist. One can either be a part of the problem or choose to be a part of the solution. Anat runs the education programme at the Israel-Palestine Centre for Research and Information (IPCRI), and has persevered over the last two years with a grass-roots peace group for schools which brings Israeli and Palestinian teachers together.

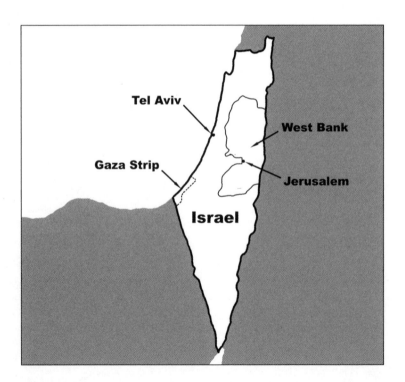

I know that ideas about peace have been running in my head since I was very young. I was recently reminded of a composition I wrote when I was 12; it was entitled 'My Disappointment', and I wrote about my disappointment in 1968 when we did not achieve peace after the '67 war. I cared about the underprivileged and I cared about marginalized parts of society. At high school I was involved in demonstrations and the students I was involved with had a clear political stance against violence and against the Israeli occupation of the Palestinian territories. We were very much for peace.

I can't say that there was a certain event or a certain situation that made me change my mind and realize that I had to act in this direction rather than others. Somehow, I have always been around these issues, although I do remember a couple of things.

First of all there was a story about a single demonstrator standing in front of the Pentagon or the White House with a sign against the war in Vietnam, and a journalist approached and said, 'Do you think you can change the system all on your own?' and the guy said, 'Well, I don't know about that, but I definitely don't want the system to change me.' From that I knew that he didn't stand alone, and secondly, I also knew that the issue was not his personal change, but the change of US policy towards Vietnam.

Another thing I remember is when I was 15 years old, my literature teacher, a little woman in her 40s with glasses and carrying a small book of poems entered the class. We didn't know at that time her name or anything else about her. She didn't say anything — she just entered and started reading a poem called 'I want to die in my bed' by Yehuda Amichai, an Israeli poet. The

desire to die in one's own bed of old age is contradictory to the
ethos of the Israeli society in the fifties, sixties and beginning of
the seventies, which was to live and die as a hero — in the
battlefield. In this way the system moulded your awareness. Ever
since, I've remembered this episode as a very powerful one, as an
episode that made me question some of 'the truths' upon which I
was raised. It was Beatles time, and it was from that time on that
I began to look critically at the way I was educated and at the way
we were taught at school — the ethos and the myth that we were
raised upon.

In the army, I used to hang signs, 'Israel and Palestine: Two states
for two nations', and things of that sort. I used to say that Israel
was coming to a point where it might lose its right to exist as a
nation state if it didn't live according to moral standards.

As a student of classical studies I worked at the archaeological
museum where I later became in charge of the education department. In 1981–82, during the war in Lebanon the gap between
studying such subjects as the life of Cicero and the poems of
Horatius and my concerns about the death that was happening in
Lebanon became irreconcilable. I stopped studying and later
resigned from my position at the museum and started working for
peace full time, at first, voluntarily, mainly with Peace Now. Later
on it became the main thing I do, at work and in my free time —
peace activist, spokesperson of MK Ran Cohen, coordinator in
New Outlook (an Israeli-Palestinian journal), coordinator of a conference of international Jewish leadership for peace, etc. Parallel
to this I continued to do work in education and became more
aware of the issue of narratives.

In 1993 I started working as the conceptual designer of the National Parks Authority in Israel and was asked to design a national park in Hammat Tiberias. The goal was to lead a team and to design the national park according to a concept. The objective was to learn the story of the place, its excavations and findings, choose an educational narrative and design the national park around this narrative. The stories that the national authorities are mainly interested in are those of the Jewish narrative and heritage. Especially whilst working on this project I started thinking more about the issue of narratives and their political contexts. Whose narratives? Whose agenda? What serves whom?

In 1996 a friend of mine called, saying, 'We're looking for directors and staff for a new peace education programme in IPCRI (Israel/Palestine Centre for Research and Information). Could you recommend someone?' So I said, 'Look, I don't want to recommend anyone. I want to do it!' That's how I found myself in 1996 working with a wonderful team lead by a warm, brilliant and professional man, Dr Marwan Derweish, who has greatly inspired me. At that time, we still had hopes about the peace process and Oslo agreement. Together, we Israelis and Palestinians, Muslims, Christians and Jews started this beautiful venture that I have been involved in until now. We were working together in one office, in one place, in East Jerusalem — which didn't feel a safe place for the Jews in the team. It was a totally new thing. Awareness of the fact that all human beings are equal and that there are no differences between nationalities is one thing. Actually working together, with all the baggage that people bring along with their different cultures and attitudes, is another.

This is a very powerful experience. I remember Nedal telling us about when he was doing his second degree in Scotland, where a family offered him a room. When he was told that a Jewish student had stayed there before him, he left the place because he couldn't imagine himself sharing a room with memories of a Jewish student! So imagine — for him it was the first time he had spoken and worked together with Israelis. For me, it hadn't been the first time I'd cooperated or worked with Palestinians, but it was the first time of doing real work together on a daily basis. It was a moulding experience, and I learned a great deal from it. After you go through a process of living and working with 'the other', and encounters with 'the other', you examine all the values you want to work on. On the one hand, you do *think* about the values you want to work on. And on the other hand, you ask yourself: do I *live* according to these values? On a daily basis you examine the narratives that you grew up with, and which you believed were true, and you look critically at the myths and truths of your life.

Today, after seven years, we have a beautiful project. There are teachers and students from 60 high schools in Israel and Palestine who participate in our programmes and who undertake training in which they go through experiences similar to the ones that we went through. Educators, as agents of change, despite the horrible situation they live in, undertake our trainings and participate in our encounters with the other, mainly because nobody can live without hope; and we, at IPCRI, a joint Israeli-Palestinian organization, offer a model that can provide it.

Once the school joins the programme, two pilot classes and four to six teachers undergo training in the curriculum. First, they implement activities and workshops about universal values: liberty, equality and social involvement.

Then they move to issues such as power relations and mechanisms of power, narratives (meta-historical) and negotiation skills — conflict resolution and so on.

The first training is held in a single identity group, after which they enter the schools to work with their students with supervision and guidance by our staff.

After about six months, the teachers participate in a joint Israeli-Palestinian encounter in which they get to know the other on a personal level and on a collective level both cultural and political.

Following the teachers' encounters, they prepare their students for a similar experience.

If they 'survive' all this, every year, they're invited to consolidate their experience and learning, and to learn another dimension of peace studies.

And the question is that if they really do internalize it, and decide to take steps to act towards change, positive change, then we have succeeded in what we do. Honestly, it took me years, first to reflect on what I do, then to ask questions about it, and finally to really internalize it. It's a very difficult process.

Funding is an issue, although not to the extent that we cannot operate, but to the extent that we cannot develop as much as we would like. For instance, 60 schools participate in our programme. Of course, in order to enlarge the impact we need to work with ten times as many schools. Further funds will enable it. I'm quite lucky because IPCRI's co-directors Dr Gershon Baskin and Dr Zakaria Qaq do most of the fund-raising and are very skilful. Yet in a paradoxical way, since the second Intifada started you hear from quite a number of organizations asking, 'What do you want funding for? You haven't done so well so far, have you?' From 1993 until 2002, $20–25 million were spent on people-to-people activities — the price of half a Merkava tank! Apparently funding weapons is much sexier than funding peace.

So far we work only in schools. The formal education system is one arena of socialization processes. Based on that assumption we are working in schools, yet next year is entitled 'from the school yard to the community' and what we are trying to do now is to move in that direction. In Israel, community work is not as developed as it is in the UK. We try to develop women's groups and parents' groups. In one of our schools next year, one of the teachers is going to implement the same programme with parents. We've just submitted a proposal for a project on human rights; students will do their activity, and work with human rights organizations that already operate in the community. So we do think about it, although we don't exactly have the key. But it's something that we want to try.

There are two things that I've been quite preoccupied with lately. The first is: how do you change people? How can you make a change in people's minds? Generally speaking, some people go through change because of one thing and some because of another. Still, I think that we have to sharpen that key and know how to use it. In a way, unless you try different keys you will not do it, and because of that we try to work on a holistic approach. We don't only work on the cognitive element. We use emotional workshops and we try many keys. Another thing I'm preoccupied with mainly today is: how do you bring about a change? What can we offer the marginalized communities, who will probably not be able to get more justice in this era of globalization, because the stronger parties will not give it of their own free will? What options do we give to the marginalized? And if we leave them without options in positive ways — in possible nonviolent ways to achieve more justice — what are we left with? Can education for peace bring about change? Can mediation and conflict resolution make a difference? It's frightening because the polarization is becoming deeper and if we don't know how to do it, if we don't know what to offer, I'm afraid we will pay a very high price.

When I started working, I learned that I wasn't so impartial. I had as many prejudices and stereotypical thoughts as other people. However, now I know how to identify them and fight against them. I learned that I wasn't as beautiful as I thought I was. But also, I have learnt that I can influence people, mainly because they know I care. So it's not only an intellectual process or a rational thing — I really care. The news is so frustrating and so horrible — when five Palestinians are killed, I immediately ask myself 'who?' They are not anonymous people but familiar faces. We have a core group of people in our programme who have worked for five or six years together and I know that whenever there is a suicide bomb there is a Palestinian group that calls me. And, of course, I do the same. It feels good that we remain human beings in all this madness around us.

I think I do what I do because I can't do otherwise. To me there are three options for coping with the situation. The first option is to close the gate so that the world will not get inside your house. But this is not possible. The outside world penetrates your life. The second option is to be a fatalist, to say, 'whatever happens, happens'. I'm not a religious person and I'm not in such deep despair to become indifferent. The third option is to do something about it. And I'm very glad that I have the opportunity to do something about it because otherwise I would go crazy. One has to choose. Either you remain a part of the problem or you choose to become a part of the solution. Choosing this option probably involves one's feeling better with oneself as well. That egoistic element is there all the time; you do what you do for others but you gain satisfaction and self-respect knowing you are doing something important that makes your life more meaningful. You know that you are living for something and you know that you care and that matters a lot.

But, there is a price. Whatever choice you make you pay a price. You often feel lonely in what you do. You often feel that the trend, public opinion — all the big things — they go in one direction and you go in another, and you feel alone and helpless. But then I think about the story of the single demonstrator outside the Pentagon and I know that I am going in the other way. In Israel sometimes if you're in the grocery store or the supermarket and you meet a neighbour who asks what you do and you tell them, you will be mocked or ridiculed. This is not such a high price to pay. For my daughter, there might be a higher cost because of the education she received. She refused to go into the army in Israel. She's very politically minded. If she doesn't go to jail for it she might pay a price because she may not be able to work in the educational system, she may not be able to work in the public sector — although I hope this changes. For the Palestinians it could be worse — they might be murdered.

Amjad Jaouni

Born in Jerusalem in 1962, to one of the six original Jerusalemite families, Amjad was raised in a very traditional culture and well-knit community; he had a true sense of being a Jerusalemite. He later moved to the American south-west where he studied and worked as an environmental engineer. In 1999, following the Palestinian-Israeli peace accord, Amjad decided to move back home to help build the new Palestine. However, only weeks later, the Intifada broke out. The

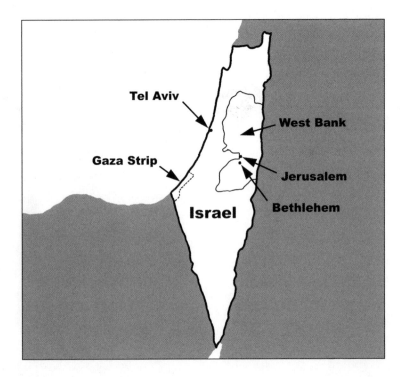

situation took a direct toll on his family, career and finances, and he was illegally stripped of his right to reside in the Holy Land. Today, he works hard pursuing the dream of a homeland.

My journey towards reconciliation work began while I was in America where I lived for 18 years. It was the time of the first Intifada, the uprising against Israeli occupation. I watched the events on TV as they unfolded — it was very painful because I felt guilty for not taking part in it and wondered every time what part would I have played if I had been there. My first opportunity to discuss my views with the opposite side was in college, but as we were both on extreme opposite ends, I thought the time I spent reading about explosives was more productive. I was harshly criticized by my Palestinian colleagues for having a discussion with an extremist. But I was not able to tell them about my preparedness to go in the other direction, which I felt would balance my approach.

Before I went to the United States, I lived in Jerusalem and attended high school during the late seventies. Israeli soldiers used to be all over the city and we, as school children, made good use of their presence to have some excitement. The scene of an army patrol chasing a student was the daily after-school routine, after which we would recover books that were dropped during the chase for safekeeping; then we would listen to their arrest and interrogation story days later when they were released.

But at that time there wasn't any large-scale violence, just small provocations, though enough warning about things to come. The underlying issues were never addressed: there was occupation. This was the same generation who started the first Intifada — youth of my age from back home. The only thing that changed is that I was away in the US, but every event shown on TV from back home had a signature of a place I had known, with a new story I was afraid to hear.

After my extended stay in the US, my family back in Jerusalem was urging me to come back home with my children; after all, there was finally peace and even career opportunities in my field. I always wanted my children to learn my culture and language but did not want them to be chased by army patrols, experience tear gas or curfews. But since all that had changed and now we had peace, I made the decision, packed, and brought the children (then aged 8, 10 and 12) home.

Ironically, only weeks after my return to Jerusalem late in 1999, the peace process stalled and the second Intifada started. The whole situation changed dramatically; I had missed the first Intifada, but now I became part of the second. Worse still, my children would have to take part in it too, like I did over 20 years ago. All those thoughts that I had had during the first Intifada flashed back: 'What am I going to do now? How am I going to react to it?' Of course, I had the option to return to the US, but I had set my heart on and directed all my energy to a future in Jerusalem, being with my family and enjoying life, whatever it might bring, in my own country — something that anyone, even in the poorest countries, takes for granted.

Soon after my return to Jerusalem, I discovered that my right to reside in my homeland was illegally revoked; I was no longer a resident because of the ethnic cleansing practices by the Israeli Ministry of Interior, laws which were retroactively implemented and designed to maintain a Jewish majority over the city where I was born. Despite the fact that my three children had been registered as legal residents a few years back, I had to re-enter as a tourist to be with them, in my home town and my city of birth, three months at a time for the past three years. Every three months when I re-enter, I look at the faces of 'Olim': Jews who have the 'natural' right to immigrate to Israel, encouraged by the state, only because they are Jews.

I returned to Jerusalem because I wanted to take part in the building of my country, but I soon found that I was witnessing its destruction right before my eyes. Our incompetent leadership was partly to blame because they had no true convictions of peace and they reacted to a counterpart who did not want peace either. It takes a lot of courage to be an initiator, especially at a time when our whole population is hostage to extremists and leaders on both sides. In fact, the extremists are in a minority and during the peace process they did not have a strong voice, but now they have taken the lead, so the situation has deteriorated drastically. I felt powerless and had to decide what I could do.

At the time I was working with the United Nations Development Programme (UNDP) and was managing an environmental programme for the Israel/Palestine Centre for Research and Information (IPCRI), which is a public policy think-tank devoted to developing practical solutions to the Israeli-Palestinian conflict. The IPCRI programme was about mediating environmental disputes between Israelis and Palestinians. But as the conflict situation worsened, we had to do more work on the people's issues. This is because although our ostensible subject matter is to do with the environment, we are bringing Palestinians and Israelis together and getting to know each other on a personal level. Many of the Palestinians had not had contact with Israelis before so this was a unique experience for them. The meetings turned out to be more of a challenge because we could not find a place in Israel or Palestine where it was logistically possible or even safe for both sides to meet, so we fly them to Turkey. Even in Turkey, conflict news makes its way from home and that disrupts work that we are trying to do in isolation from such influence.

Our work is about trying to bring people together in a situation where the extremists seem to have the upper hand. This extremism is fed by what the children are taught at an early age — two nations wanting to send each other into the sea, exile, diaspora, refugee camps, ethnic transfer, etc. Palestinian children have always learned: 'A bird's home is called a nest, a lion's home is called a den. My home is called Palestine, from the river to the sea.' Similarly, Israeli children are taught that they are God's chosen people, and God has promised them my land, and that a non-Jew is a second-class human being. Both grow up to believe that the entire country is theirs alone, and that the other side does not have a face or a name.

One thing IPCRI did was to set up 'virtual' dialogues/encounters between Palestinian and Israeli schoolchildren. A group of 15 elementary schoolchildren aged 13–16 from two different schools (a Palestinian school in Bethlehem and an Israeli school in

Kiryat Gat) discussed and chatted about the issues on the Internet. The conversations were so intelligent — I wish we had those kids as our leaders! There were no arguments of 'which came first, the chicken or the egg?' or in our case what started the Intifada, or what stopped the peace process. They addressed the issues that we have to deal with now, how to ensure that this happens or that doesn't happen so that there can be a compromise.

Successes like the virtual encounters sometimes do not make it that far, as the media on both sides pay more attention to conflict. For example, CNN News was supposed to cover the virtual encounters, but that very same morning an Israeli bus was bombed. The media just covered the bombing and no one knew that Palestinian and Israeli children were actually discussing peace together, at exactly the same moment. There are terrorists on both sides, but the media often gets to decide.

Prior to the Intifada there was plentiful funding for such activities. But when the situation became less peaceful, these supporters reduced or even eliminated funding — exactly the opposite of what they should have done — so we are trying to do much needed activities with less available resources. It is like rolling a large boulder uphill.

Adapting to the situation is a challenge. For example, after the outbreak of the Intifada, IPCRI had to move its offices from Bethlehem to a place on a hill that is accessible from both Jerusalem and the West Bank city of Bethlehem through an unpaved rocky road not far from an army checkpoint. My colleagues Sirin and Eisha (a Christian woman and a Muslim woman) come from Bethlehem along that road every day in order to bypass the army checkpoint: Sirin, who is a charming, witty lady, manages to make her way through, even during clashes in the area. Eisha, who comes from a refugee camp near Bethlehem, takes that same route after taking her children (by hand, for safety) to school, but she gets noticed more often with the traditional scarf she wears on her head. When that happens she either gets turned back, humiliated or on occasions beaten by the soldiers. Eisha attempts to persuade the soldiers by telling them where she works, but often ends up calling Gershon (who is the Israeli co-director of IPCRI) who engages the soldiers who take him seriously because he is an Israeli.

Gershon himself has to fetch his daughter every day from school because suicide bombers blow up the Israeli buses. He had his car torched in east Jerusalem once because someone knew he was an Israeli. He wore a Palestinian headscarf (*kufyya*) for a while to be able to come safely to Bethlehem.

The back road near the office is a common route for Palestinian labour workers seeking employment by Israelis in Jerusalem. So it is often there where the hide-and-seek takes place between those people and the soldiers. A place on a hill also has its advantages as we hear and see the infamous clashes within bullet range. In one instance, I was surprised to see Sirin showing up at the office during the Bethlehem invasion. She had taken the near impossible mission of going to Jerusalem in the middle of street shootings, a curfew and a complete city closure in order to buy medication for her grandfather who suffered from a heart condition. I thought it would be the last time I saw her alive as she attempted to take the medicine back into Bethlehem where her grandfather lived not far from the Church of the Nativity. She cried as she held the medicine and said: 'I don't know what I would do if my grandfather dies; I would …' My thoughts then were that if anyone is hurt so much and willing to take such a risk, they could have taken that journey to execute a suicide bombing, even under the strictest curfew and city closure. There were many tragedies which I heard of that took place during the Intifada, and which were more touching than Sirin's journey. But I learned the concept from Sirin's little incident: if someone believes that they will be pushed and stepped on, in a little corner, until they die, then they will want to die there and then and they will take a few people with them if they can. This is today's suicide bomber's reality.

As for me, I struggle daily with the obstacle course of army checkpoints on my way to and from work. There is a checkpoint very near my house, and the constant, 24-hour amplified sounds from there resemble a Nazi concentration camp. Last year I was hospitalized for sunstroke, which I suffered whilst waiting in a long line at another checkpoint between Jerusalem and Ramallah; I had to take part in facilitating one of the virtual student encounters from hospital.

This is an email that I sent to a friend following a visit to Ramallah:

Yesterday I went to Ramallah during the curfew-lifting hours to see for myself the latest achievement of the IDF (Israeli Defence Force); it clearly belongs in the Halls of Shame. Shopkeepers and owners of offices in the centre of Ramallah were busy trying to secure their property. Imagine someone taking a joyride in a 50-tonne tank stepping over cars, pavements, road-signs, traffic lights, walls, shop-fronts — that is the way it was in Ramallah, multiplied by 150. Shops were looted, telephone lines, booths and electric poles were strewn in the streets. The IDF left such a barbaric scene — some areas looked so different I could not remember what was there before.

Only food shops were open, store signs and window curtains were dangling from buildings, people were rushing and getting into shops and taxis in a mechanical way; the only talk when two met was about who was arrested and who was released. In the limited time I had I went to check on a friend whom I could not contact by phone. The IDF entered many homes, and blew up with explosives doors where no one could answer the door. My friend's door was blown up because he was not there — [he was] taking shelter somewhere.

Many stores were looted by the IDF, especially easy-to-carry valuables, and mobile telephone and gift stores. They are not as valuable as the real-estate loot of 1948, but make a good gift to a family member who shares the same values, maybe a mother or a father — who else would raise children that way? I heard a baker say he sold to many people on credit because 'banks were closed'. He said the IDF paid him a visit and dumped kerosene in a big batch of dough he'd prepared — a soldier made a joke about it in a Russian language as he was pouring the kerosene in the dough. I had to leave Ramallah in a rush because it was time for the IDF armoured personnel carriers and IDF snipers to take positions in town. Next time I will check on an apartment I have in Ramallah. What can be worse? I have witnessed three wars in my 39 years, and it is now the time to take my children to show them what has happened in Ramallah.

Back to the checkpoint near my house; another porous component in the security fence surrounding Jerusalem, as the daily scene is of people bypassing it mostly for humanitarian purposes or for seeking work. Most of those people will be stopped while using public transportation, then humiliated, fined and turned back at best. Bullets are fired from the checkpoint on occasions, but twice the pattern was different, and I later learnt that people were killed. On both occasions, by a horrible irony, I was working on two portals called Place-for-Peace and Our Shared Environment, and I just continued working fearing to enquire about what happened. When someone is shot at a checkpoint no one is allowed near the person, so they bleed to death. My son witnessed a part of an incident and came home to describe to me what happened, and lay down to demonstrate how the person who was shot was moving.

Not long ago was the Muslim Eid, the Feast of Sacrifice. Israeli police vehicles were spread out having a feast of another kind, issuing traffic violations and setting up roadblocks in what was clearly a deliberate way to spoil the celebrations, as most people drive to visit relatives and go on trips. But with the city closures there are very few places to go, and very few relatives you can visit — after all, each checkpoint takes about 30 minutes to pass, and there is a checkpoint every few kilometres. My young daughter Sarah sat opposite me while I was working on my PC and said: 'Why don't they let us go?' (meaning Israelis) 'Why don't they go away?' And started crying and saying: 'I hate them, I hate them, I hate them.'

Some people are inspired by their own faith, but I look at it from a very simple perspective. I don't want my children to live in this environment, and I don't want my life to be affected by it. I just want peace based on equality. The example of trust and friendship that we have been able to nurture in small groups is what inspires me. When the bus bombing occurred moments before the student Virtual Encounters, the kids still went ahead with the dialogues (initially the Palestinian kids heard the blast and thought a Palestinian building had been bombed, but then all knew exactly what happened as they were working on the internet). There were no recriminations and they didn't try to avoid painful subjects; they continued talking about going forward, unlike our leaders. The only reason those children reacted differently to adults is that they knew kids on the other sides, simply from visiting their websites and knowing their names and seeing their photos. It is incidents like this that should inspire politicians.

I think most people, both Palestinians and Israelis, are fooling themselves about finding a practical solution. For example, many Palestinians consider Gershon (the Israeli co-director of IPCRI) to be a supporter and advocate of the Palestinian cause and as having moderate views, whilst they consider Zakaria (the Palestinian co-director, who advocates exactly the same principles) to be someone with undesirable views. We have seen the Israeli-Palestinian conflict as 'us and them' but we have never looked at it as a conflict.

Most people I know consider reconciliation work as something in the wrong direction, and despite all the hard work these efforts go unnoticed; the immediate rewards are so little and the risks are many. It is very difficult to pursue this work and attempt to isolate one's thoughts from the conflict.

Caoimhe Butterly

Caoimhe Butterly was born in Dublin, Ireland in 1978. When she was eight months old her family moved to Canada, then to Mauritius when she was twelve and two years later to Zimbabwe. She became involved in work with Aids patients there, and spent some months working in a mission hospital in rural Zimbabwe before her 'A' levels. Instead of

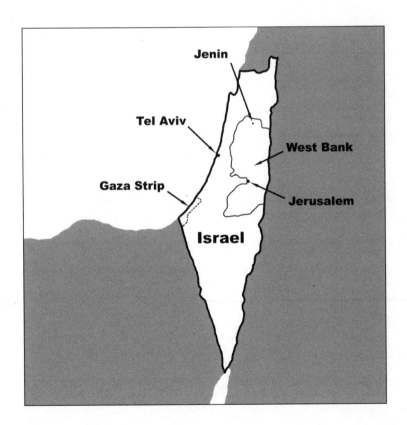

going into higher education she chose to experience the world. She went to New York where she worked for the Catholic Worker Movement. From there she went to Guatemala and Mexico, spending two years with the Zapatistas. In 2001 Caoimhe returned to Ireland. The same year, in protest to the Irish Government's decision to allow American planes heading for Afghanistan to refuel at Shannon Airport, she fasted for ten days outside the Department of Foreign Affairs. After being arrested for blocking the runway when the war started, she left for Iraq to work with an activist group opposing sanctions. She then moved to work in Palestine. In 2003 she returned to Iraq and is, at the time of writing, in India.

Caiomhe Butterly is featured in the cover photo of this book, walking up to a tank in Jenin. We tried to contact her to ask her to write her own story as most other contributors have done. However it proved impossible to reach her, since the places she has been have been inaccessible to 'normal' communications. Therefore we have put together a brief story about her, with the help of articles by Katie Barlow, Michael McCaughan and Caoimhe herself, to whom we are most grateful. Full references for their articles appear at the end of the story.

It was in April 2002 that the world first noticed Caoimhe Butterly. She smuggled herself into Yasser Arafat's compound in Ramallah to help a wounded Palestinian friend after the Israeli Defence Forces (IDF) had denied access to the Red Crescent. Caoimhe, a young Irish human rights activist, had been staying in Jenin since late 2001 as an international observer.

During the 12 days she was stuck in the compound (the IDF refused to let her out) the tanks closed in on Jenin and when she finally managed to escape she found death and destruction. Fifty-nine people had died, many were injured. She helped the survivors find the bodies of the loved ones by digging in the rubble by hand, recovering body parts and children.

On 23 November 2002 Caoimhe hit the headlines again. An Israeli soldier shot her in the thigh while she was helping some children take refuge in alleyways. This was no surprise to her. She had been almost expecting it. A couple of months earlier Caoimhe had been pleased to meet Katie Barlow, a journalist who stayed with her for two weeks to shoot a documentary. Caoimhe wanted somebody to record her story in case something happened to her.

The April events in Jenin rendered her fearless and had given her sheer determination to remain in Jenin to help the Palestinians. She walked up to tanks, confronted soldiers, stood in the line of fire and shielded old people and children with her body while the Red Crescent took them to hospital. Caoimhe also chose not to speak about her experience in Ramallah and thereafter, fearing that she would have been deported.

With time Caoimhe noted that IDF had increasingly become intolerant of her presence. As this happened, concerned that her confrontational style could have heightened military brutality to civilians, she changed tactics and focused on helping people in their daily lives. She felt that accompanying people in their day-to-day business was the most effective use of her presence. It enabled people to resist the attempt of the IDF to destroy community life through uncertainty and unpredictability. Katie Barlow recalls her words: '… never knowing when the next tank will invade, or bullet will be fired'.

Caoimhe abhors violence. Her young life has been committed to finding ways forward beyond the mire of violence. She believes that the pursuit of a daily routine despite the 'intrusion' of the military and tanks is the best form of resistance for the Palestinians. 'I have reservations on what forms of resistance should be used, but I do believe the Palestinians have a right to resist, and that oppressed people have a right to resist. But I think some of the means employed here are sometimes strategically and ethically misguided,' she told Katie Barlow. Nonviolence has to be the way. In order not to be defeated, the community had to continue its daily existence. The Palestinians have decided to counteract military action by continuing to take their children to school, by going to mosques, to work and to the marketplace. This is how Katie recalls Jenin: '… one minute a fully functional buzzing town, minutes later people are running for cover'.

Then November came. The 23rd was an intense day. The IDF had been entering Jenin yet again, with tanks, armed personnel carriers (APC, a vehicle similar to a tank without the cannon), helicopters, and jeeps. Men had been arrested. The UNRWA (United Nations Relief Works Agency) had been trying to negoti- ate a safe passage away from the UN compound for their Palestinian workers and some children and women who had been there for a vaccination programme. Despite the fighting and the injured, ambulances were impeded from passing. Caoimhe had been called to where some children had gathered. She saw a tank approach and tried to dissuade the soldiers from shooting at unarmed children. Then an APC came. She could see the soldiers' faces. One of the soldiers took his rifle and shot, first in the air then lowered his aim. Caoimhe was clearing some children from the road into the alley when she was shot. She fell and as she dragged herself into the alley bullets flew at close range. She is sure she was visible enough for the soldier to see her.

Despite this she was still keen to stay. 'I'm going nowhere. I'm staying until this occupation ends. I have the right to be here, a responsibility to be here. So does anyone who knows what is going on here. I'm going nowhere. I understand the need to balance my own precious life with the need to stand up for those who have no voice.' This was what Caoimhe told Katie Barlow from her hospital bed.

Caoimhe is motivated by a strong sense of social justice and of responsibility towards those who need help. This sense of duty has characterized her since an early age. 'I've always felt the compulsion, to an almost painful degree, of needing to stand up against injustices in whatever contexts they lie, in whatever context I am living.' As a child she was always interested in the environment and in helping people — particularly the mentally handicapped. Caoimhe became interested at a young age in Nelson Mandela.

Her relentless campaigning for human rights has been deeply inspired by the culture of liberation theology (a Christian movement which advocates compassion and leadership in the struggle against injustice and poverty) in which she was brought up. Another important influence was the work of Dorothy Day, founder of Catholic Worker Movement. She encountered this thinking while working in the Movements' soup kitchens in New York after she left school. Day's motto was: 'Comfort the afflicted and afflict the comfortable'.

Michael McCaughan, a journalist who met Caoimhe in Mexico while she was working with the Zapatistas, recalls her spirit of adaptation and sacrifice. She is 'a real leader', Caoimhe's mother had told him. 'She believes everyone can make a difference.'

A year later Caoimhe wrote from Iraq. 'I have confronted death so many times now, of friends, of those around me, in Zimbabwe, in Latin America, in Jenin, that I do not fear it. I am afraid however of a senseless death, a stray or intended bullet, I want desperately — as so do most human beings — to live, to love, to continue to struggle, to resist the policies and practices that deny so many people the right to live with dignity. [...] This is what keeps me here. I fluctuate between fear and a crystal clarity that there is no other place I should be now. That witnessing and accompanying, and supporting the emergence of a nonviolent resistance movement here is vital [...], that a front-line is never an easy but sometimes necessary place to inhabit.'

Sources

Barlow, K., 'Courage Under Fire', in *The Guardian,* 27 November 2002.

Barlow, K., 'West Bank Hero', in *Sunday Business Post,* 8 December 2002.

Butterly, C., 'I Was Shot Escorting Jenin's School Children', in *Counterpunch,* 23 November 2002.

Butterly, C., 'Iraq: The Things That Keep Us Here', in *Electronic Iraq,* 18 August 2003.

McCaughan, M., 'Front Line Life of an Irish Peace Crusader', in *The Observer,* 7 April 2002.

Maria Mangte

Maria Mangte, whose original name is Lingbhoi, comes from the north-east of India — the province of Manipur, which borders Burma (Myanmar), Thailand and China. Until 50 years ago the tribes in the area lived side by side in peace despite all the differences, and even lived partly together. Then British colonization and Christian missionaries affected their cultural heritage. They were followed by businessmen, plantation founders, and soldiers, because north-east India is rich in mineral resources, tropical woods and fertile highland soil. Tribal

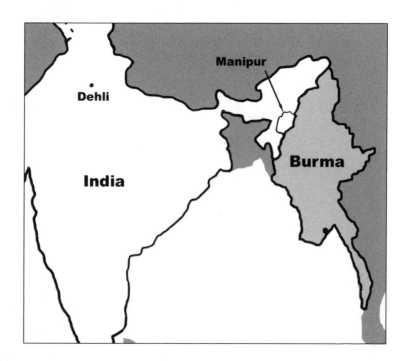

communities were torn apart and in the struggle Maria lost her
parents, husband and two children to inter-tribal warfare. She has
overcome great personal difficulties in order to advance peaceful
resolutions amongst indigenous people. She was completely unlettered
but is now one of the few women members of a council that represents
tribal peoples in India.

I have been at the centre of conflict for most of my life. I come
from the province of Manipur in north-east India on the borders
of Burma, Thailand and China, where there has long been resistance to the central government. Many inhabitants still belong to
indigenous tribes. Until about 50 years ago, they lived together
harmoniously, but the central government used a strategy of
'divide and rule' and set the tribes against each other. I belong to
a small community called 'KOM'. We are small in numbers and
are now almost extinct, but our community stands neutral
between two warring communities. Both tried to claim our tribe
which was dangerous for us because we were split into two
groups — one lobbying for the Tankhuls and the other for the
Kukis. To try to stop this communal struggle within my
community was challenging and dangerous. I was also drawn in
different directions within myself. I had had a Christian education
in a convent school but, through my grandmother, I inherited
some of our tribal culture. From her, I learned the ways of
preserving and guarding nature; much of the work my
grandmother did was done in secret, because it was seen as
witchcraft. We were all connected to nature, and the community

in itself was in harmony. We did not know a God who stood above all things. From my father I inherited Western values — education, culture and a desire for political participation and decision-making. He became a resistance fighter who was persecuted by the government and spent a large part of his life in jail.

It was while I was at school that I was awakened to social problems, when I used to accompany the nuns in their fieldwork in remote villages. This was where I learned to live a good Christian life, learning to give and help and to forgive and pray. But this also led me into political activism. When I was at college I became a student leader and later I joined the revolutionary movement, the People's Liberation Army (PLA). We were fighting for the freedom of Manipur state and to bring social justice to our society. We wanted to get rid of gender inequality, nepotism and corruption, discrimination on the basis of religion or caste, and economic disparity. All I knew at this time was the poverty of the people and their oppression, and all my thoughts were about how to liberate them. As a young woman, I worked in the resistance with my husband and most of the people in my village. During the armed struggle, many were killed, including my husband. I was able to flee and managed to move to Delhi, where I studied politics. I kept my identity secret, as I would have been seen as the wife of a terrorist.

My political activities included a march to China (in 1979) when I was the only girl among hundreds of boys. Our hope was to establish links with the Chinese Government and to seek assistance in support of our movement. We wanted to establish a strong base at the border to fight the Indians following

Communist ideology. My role was to be guide, nurse, motivator and interpreter. Later, I found that most of the cadres were not politically conscious. Many hailed from poor families, with neither jobs nor education, and I realized that they had nothing else to do but take up rifles since they did not fit in anywhere.

Eventually, I became disillusioned with the revolutionary movement. I found there the same nepotism, power politics and hierarchical authority that I had opposed in the mainstream government. The Chinese Government had changed its policies of giving outside support, but more importantly, I could not accept communist brainwashing tactics or reconcile communist teachings with my Christian background. The purpose of being a revolutionary was defeated when I found the normal tendency to selfishness and greed within the group. So, in 1984, I returned to India. I travelled through the jungles of Burma (as it then was), but when I reached Manipur, the Manipur state police arrested me on a variety of criminal charges and handed me over to the Indian army.

Detention in the army camp was an important turning-point in my life. I faced intensive interrogation from officials from the state central intelligence (CID) and the military intelligence (MI) and sometimes from the press. But this experience completely changed my impressions of the Indian army. Contrary to what I had thought, I found them gentle and polite when they spoke to me, and generally respectful of women. They tried to understand my views and to comprehend the situation as I described the cultural diversity within the area and the differences from the mainstream. They willingly accepted many of my views on social and economic problems, although we could not agree on political matters. But whatever the case, I wanted to be neutral between the two sides and was willing to do anything to bridge the gap between the Indian army and the rebels and to bring them to the negotiating table if possible. My life too was at stake. I knew that if I did not prove myself, I would not be released and nor would the groups let me live in peace.

In 1968, I agreed to go back to the rebels of the PLA on a special mission. I had a message from the Indian Government for peace talks and political negotiations. Once more I crossed the border into Burma and went to the headquarters of the Kachin Independence Organization (KIO), where I met the chairman Mr Maran Branseng. I discussed my mission with him as a special messenger to the rebels for peace talks. Contact was made with the PLA, but there was no positive response. However, I came back as an emissary of the KIO with a letter addressed to the then Prime Minister of India, Mr Rajiv Gandhi, and thus left a diplomatic link between the Government of India and the KIO who were fighting for independence from the Burmese military regime.

For the next few years I led a more 'normal' life. I continued my studies in New Delhi at the Jawaharlal Nehru University. I also took a part-time job as a tour operator, which enabled me to get back to Thailand and meet KIO leaders again. I continued to act as liaison between the Kachins and the Indian authorities, simply as a humanitarian supporter of the Kachin cause, not as an Indian national. Later, I lived for a while in Thailand where I taught in a Catholic school and then worked in a finance company.

Life in Thailand was completely different from life in India. The cities were more developed than in my country and the people were friendlier and more sober, polite and gentle. I had no fears living there. I started to make a new life, earning more money than I needed, but still wanting to earn more to fulfil many dreams I had. But this desire to make more money almost destroyed my inner peace. I was suddenly moving in a different social crowd and like most normal young people I looked for entertainment in discotheques, parties and night-clubs. But I soon tired of the artificial love and romances of Thai night-life, the competitiveness and the constant race against time. It was certainly a different way of life, from the jungles to the city! But despite all the rich food and comforts, I was never really happy. I felt lonely and empty, I was worried and discontented, and frightened that I was losing something though I did not know what.

An inexplicable impulse brought me back to India (in 1993) where I worked as a project officer for the International Trade Fair Promotion Organization and then as a manager at Reebok International India. Then, once again, the whole course of my life was changed. I was working in Delhi, but I was soon confronted with the victims of the ethnic conflict that was flaring up in my region.

Many displaced women were coming to Delhi in search of relatives who could offer them shelter and moral support, and many of them ended up on my doorstep. I listened to their stories about the war that had suddenly interrupted without rhyme or reason. Their sufferings were not only physical. There was the mental trauma and sorrows of parting from loving neighbours from other communities because of the ethnic violence. It was the women and children who were most vulnerable and this affected me too. I became once more a changed person thinking, 'This could be me.'

The situation back in my region was getting worse. Many women were destitute having become widows while the men fought in inter-tribal wars. Many orphaned children were begging in the streets with no homes to go to. Young people were taking drugs, young girls were going into prostitution, and many had become HIV positive. There was increased crime and extortion, while insurgency led to military operations and atrocities to suppress the insurgency. Many women and girls were raped by the soldiers. So this was when I started engaging in relief work, trying to find solutions to the social problems. The first step was to provide immediate relief to the victims of conflict in terms of shelter, food and clothing, and we hoped that the trouble would end soon.

I soon found that relief work was not enough. The victims were beginning to develop a 'dependency syndrome' because there was nothing for them to do in the towns and cities. This was not their fault. They had come from villages where they were able to grow their own food in the forestlands and to be self-sufficient. But in the towns they were forced to live on charity, which was degrading to them. We needed to initiate income-generating activities and at first the most obvious thing was to encourage women to use their traditional cloth-weaving skills which are rare and in danger of vanishing. For weeks at a time we searched the city for markets where we could sell this traditional tribal clothing.

I also worked at the political level to promote the resolution of ethnic conflicts, so that displaced people could return to their homes and normal life. For this work, the Tribal Welfare Society came into existence. The society worked holistically to cater to the needs of victims and other downtrodden people in society. It contributed to education and health needs, provided legal aid, and promoted income-generating projects. It also raised awareness about peace, conflict resolution and human rights issues.

As a result of this work, I became involved in organizations at the national level devoted to promoting the interests and welfare of tribal peoples. In 1994, I was appointed Joint Secretary of the All India Tribal Development Council, and in 1996 I was elected as Secretary General of the Indian Confederation of Indigenous and Tribal Peoples. In 1997, I was a representative at the UN Working Group on Indigenous Peoples held in Geneva. There I met representatives from all the revolutionary groups in our region. With all their different goals and objectives, they were seeking support from the Western world for their movements. At this conference, we wanted to raise awareness and understanding amongst our European supporters of the problems we faced and the gravity of the situation.

Working for peace in a conflict zone is not easy with so many diverse ethnic communities who are rivals to each other. The situation is so confusing it is difficult to know what to do. Every well-intentioned action can invite hatred and suspicion, because if you work with one community another will consider you an enemy. The best approach is to find problems shared by the same kinds of people from different groups. For example, we work with women from different groups who have been victims of violence, or we try to bring traditional leaders together to discuss common problems, or we try to bring together unemployed youths from different communities. There are all kinds of practical activities that can bring people together, like the women's weaving project or agricultural projects, as well as seminars and workshops.

My experiences as a student leader, as a revolutionary, as a political prisoner, as a social worker and as a movement leader have taught me that the 'grass is not greener on the other side'. I have decided to work for peace and my work is to build bridges where peoples have been torn apart. I also realize that no liberation movement can bring freedom or liberate the human race. Freedom is in the minds and hearts of people. This taught me to respect every individual in their own place, which brought a feeling of stillness and peace in the middle of a noisy crowd. I understood that we need to create many more visionaries and not merely leaders. It just needs a human heart to touch the souls of those who are suffering and peace is within you. And inward peace will bring peace to the outside world. Working for peace is not easy and we are often misunderstood, but it is not an impossible task either when everyone joins hands to work for peace.

Ben Mussanzi wa Mussangu

Ben Mussanzi Wa Mussangu originally studied economic sciences and radiography in Zaire. His employment at the missionary CME (Centre Medical Evangelique) hospital led to his returning to university to study medicine and become a doctor. These plans were interrupted by the events of 10 May 1990, after which he was employed by a missionary hospital where he succeeded in reconciling three Anglican

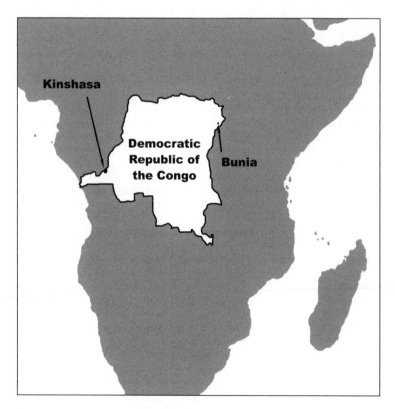

bishops who had been in conflict for more than ten years. Following this experience, he returned to the Congo, and worked again in the local hospital when clashes between the tribes broke out. At this point he decided to concentrate on peace work, which led to his founding the Centre Résolution Conflits (CRC), and the extraordinary work he is doing.

How did I become a peacemaker today?

The story starts in the early nineties just before the Rwandan genocide. I'm a radiology technician. I studied radiology in the Institute Superieur des Techniques Medicales (ISTM) at the University of Kinshasa and in 1979 I was employed as radiographer by the missionary CME Hospital of Nyankunde-Bunia, Democratic Republic of Congo (DRC). In October 1980, I married Kongosi and we had four children. We have also been taking care of two orphans.

In 1984, the hospital management committee sent me for medical studies in Kisangani and later in Lubumbashi. These studies were interrupted by the incident of 10 May 1990 (killings of students), and this sad event gave us, me, the opportunity of being employed as a radiographer for two years (from 1990 to 1992) by the missionary hospital of Shyira in Rwanda. At that time, war had already broken out between the government and the 'Front Populaire Rwandais' (FPR). The strange thing was that during these two years, the Lord strongly used us, Kongosi and me, not only in the hospital but also as 'international evangelists and mediators'. This is how, on 6 June 1992, God used me to bring about the reconciliation of three Anglican bishops who had been living in conflict for ten years. After this amazing feat, that same week during our family worship I had a special message from the Lord: 'Mussanzi, I brought you to Rwanda not to carry out X-rays but to bring about the reconciliation between these bishops. Well done! Now it is time to go back to the Congo, where I have a special ministry for you.'

It was not easy to leave, as church leaders of Rwanda appreciated our faithful work both in the hospital and the church, but finally they allowed us to leave and we returned to the Congo/Zaire, where we were employed again, Kongosi as administrator and later as Internal Auditor, and I as radiographer at the Nyankunde hospital.

I was nearly killed by my own tribe

But only six months after our coming back and just when we had settled there, ethnic clashes began around the hospital in which many lives were lost. The clashes were between our own Ngiti tribe and the neighbouring Hema ethnic group (this was in December 1992). The reason I got into this new field was twofold. Firstly, we couldn't get any sleep with CME Nyankunde hospital colleagues. After working hard during the day, we were called again every night at any time when new casualties arrived from different villages. Secondly, I was nearly killed by my own tribe because they thought that I was from another group. This kind of error is the terrible tragedy of any war, that so often people who have harmed nobody are killed. I came upon this group by the river where they had set up an ambush for some people in another group. I tried to explain to them — in our own language — who I was, and they said, 'No, we don't believe you. Now everyone knows this language — you are from another group.' If I'm alive today, it's a miracle from God!

This is how it happened. I had been talking to these people for two hours trying to convince them. It was noon and in Africa it gets very hot, and after two hours trying to convince these people my saliva finally dried up and I was not able to open my mouth. Finally, I closed my eyes saying in my mind, 'My goodness, how can I convince these people?' And when I closed my eyes, I saw red. In Africa, especially in our area, there is a superstition according to which, when you are attacked by enemies and close your eyes, you are in trouble if you see red. That red is a sign of blood — so I began to tremble. Before that, I had the courage to stand up to them. The only thing I remember is saying (in my mind because I couldn't open my lips), 'Lord, open my lips just to say a last thing to these people.' And my lips opened. So I said to these people, 'Before you kill me, please just allow me to pray' (because I am a Christian).

These people had taken drugs — in these ethnic conflicts people take drugs in order to be able to kill without pity. Ethnic conflicts are the worst ones, as the person who is about to kill you might be one of your friends, who has changed his mind because of the war; or their children might have played with yours; or they know where you would be hiding, as they know all your secrets. So these men were drugged in order to be able to kill even people they knew. Their eyes were red. When I asked if I could pray, they said, 'Yes, you can pray! Maybe you are going to hell, but you can pray!' I plucked up courage and began to pray. My lips were opened and I prayed for (I think) 20 seconds and I said, 'Lord thank you. You have planned for me to be killed by my own tribe, and I pray for them. Forgive them for they don't know what they are doing, killing somebody they don't know. They don't know who I am. I've done them no harm. But they are going to kill me soon. The only thing I'm afraid of now, Lord, is that they will be in conflict within their own community. Before, they were fighting against others, now they will be fighting against themselves, because when my family members hear that I have been killed in this village, they will fight against this village. I'm afraid for them — forgive them in Jesus' name. Amen.'

Then from what I remember, I fell down and lost consciousness. From that I discovered something: when you are in trouble you can be killed, but it will be when your spirit has gone already. I sat down, and lost consciousness without even being touched. Then a miracle took place. When my consciousness came back, I found these people arguing amongst themselves: 'You see, this man must really be from our tribe. You see now he's dead. We didn't kill him. What are we going to do now?' They were accusing each other: 'You are the one who refused to let him go free.' And that made me smile. Somebody saw that I was smiling and said, 'No, he is not dead.' So quickly, they came to help me saying, 'Are you OK?'

They untied me (by the way, during these two hours, they had tied me up with my own shirt) and put my shirt back on and said,

'You can go, and please do not forget to eat white chicken, as you are lucky!' In Africa, white chicken is a symbol of good luck.

You'll be my witness in Jerusalem

The first intimation that I should work for peace and reconciliation came as I rode home. I was on my bike, praying (with my eyes open — I think the best prayer is the one done by someone in trouble with open eyes). I asked God a question: 'My Lord, I want to find a way to help these people who are killing each other out of ignorance. We can never live without others in this world, never! We need each other. I am now ready to help my people, but what can I do?' The second intimation came six months later when I had actually forgotten asking that question. We were in the church with my wife. She was seated on the left side as usual. In Protestant churches particularly, people preach long sermons, so I was sleepy. In the middle of the sermon, I felt someone touch my right knee. I asked my wife, 'Did you touch me?' and she said, 'No.' I looked to the person on my right (I didn't know him) and asked, 'Did you touch me?' and he replied, 'No.' I thought: it must be an angel. So I focused my attention on the preacher. I found this man reading — just reading — a passage from the Bible in the book of the Acts of the Apostles, chapter 1, verse 8, where Jesus before his ascension was saying to his disciples, 'You'll be my witnesses in Jerusalem, in all Judaea, in Samaria, and to the ends of the earth.' But when the preacher was explaining the meaning of this passage he said, 'It is not the Jerusalem in Israel that he means. Jerusalem is your own family, village or your own people.'

When he said that, I remembered straightaway that moment on my bike six months earlier when I had asked God 'What can I do for my people?' And an internal voice (what Christians call the 'Holy Spirit') said clearly within me, 'Mussanzi, this is a message for you. Your Jerusalem is your own tribe. You must begin here any effort to change the mentality of people who are killing each other. If you obey, I will use you later as a peace-maker and finally you will help people in conflict all over the world.' When we got back, I told my wife, 'From now on I will be going every weekend to Ngiti territory (my Jerusalem) to pass on to them messages of peace and reconciliation.' She laughed saying, 'Are you crazy? I will never allow you to go into that risky and dangerous area.' But I replied, 'No — this is a special message I got today in answer to my question of six months ago. I prefer to obey the Holy Spirit of God instead of you.'

So my wife and I were in conflict before she could understand that God himself was behind me. This was the beginning of what is known today in the north-eastern part of the DRC as *Centre Résolution Conflits* of Nyankunde-Bunia.

Foundation of the *Centre Résolution Conflits* of Nyankunde-Bunia

The Centre was founded in 1993, and by 1997 it was a fully funded formal organization based in the DRC. To put it simply, we are training people to understand that we must learn to live together. It is not easy to talk about 'peace' because it is such a huge issue. A state of peace is like a state of good health and when there is no peace, it is like a sickness. But to treat the sickness, we have to think more specifically. We have to train people how to resolve the ordinary conflicts of life that arise out of misunderstandings. When people do fight, we help them to understand the causes and the processes of conflict — at the domestic level, the community level, the national level and the international level. Above all, we teach people that there must be time to talk about problems whenever they arise.

In the beginning, we were starting from zero and having to work by trial and error. So at first we just concentrated on the people of my own tribe, the Ngiti/Lendu. For about three years, we were working on this one group because my own tribe was known in the Congo as a very dangerous tribe — very kind people but ready to kill when they are provoked. This is the result of a lot of aggression they have experienced in the past. There is what we call in conflict management 'natural aggression' and 'acquired aggression'. Let us use an illustration. In Africa, for example, there are many neglected or uncontrolled dogs running in the streets alone and children throw stones at these dogs. As a result you find dogs that were originally kind becoming aggressive. It's the same for us human beings. When you are provoking somebody all the time, even at the domestic level — it could be your partner, your wife or your husband or your children — in the end these persons will become aggressive. Many things have happened to these Lendu people in the past and, as a result, they have finally become aggressive today. It is not a justification of their killings but a theoretical explanation of what is happening in the Ituri District.

Ten years ago, in 1993, we started our peace work by training community elders, church and non-governmental organizations (NGOs) and political leaders. But three years ago, in 2000, we realized that we were not going about things the best way. We were training old people and forgetting the youth, those who would be leading the country in the future. We needed to spread training more widely. So we started a campaign to introduce conflict management courses into the curriculum of universities and colleges of the north-eastern DRC. In fact, the idea came in 1997, when I took part in a 'Working with Conflict' course organized by Responding to Conflict (RTC) at the Quaker Centre in Birmingham. Once back in the DRC, we adapted the course to our southern situation of Africa. In the beginning it was a very challenging task to convince people at home, but now, three years later, many colleges and universities have agreed to put on our conflict management course. The course is offered as a module of 30 hours' teaching and it is offered to all students in their final year. We do believe in the CRC that it's very important to reach university students because the militias are often led by people with professional training but with no moral or spiritual education. This is why the CRC has a big project of founding a Pan-African Peace University in 2007.

Outcomes of our peace work

Firstly, it's amazing to see how positively students are reacting to our training. I remember one occasion from my own teaching experience. The course had come to an end and this was the last

day of teaching. I said to my students, 'OK, the course is over —
now it's your turn to put into practice in your own lives what you
have learned and at whatever level you can.' Just as I was about to
leave, a lady started crying and asked me to come back. She said,
'All the things you have said in this course went straight to my
heart, because I was living in conflict with my neighbours.' She
stood up from her desk and went over to one of the other ladies
in the class and said, 'Please forgive me.' The teacher of the next
class was waiting outside the door, so I said to him, 'Can you lend
me your hour please? We are resolving a serious conflict here.' So
we continued for an hour of praying and healing. Each of these
ladies in conflict recognized, in front of the class, their own
responsibility.

Secondly, my wife Kongosi, who also works in peace building
and conflict resolution, has similar stories. With a colleague, she
used to visit and pray with patients twice a week in the
orthopaedic unit of the CME Nyankunde Hospital. After a short
Bible reading and comment, a young man among the patients
called out to her with tears in his eyes: 'I have to tell you
something — I was a militia fighter, and when you were speaking
I discovered that I have to confess something. I have done several
wrong things, killing people from another side that my own tribe
was in conflict with. Please can you pray for me? Do you think
that God can forgive a killer like me?' After that prayer, the young
man was healed psychologically and was able to smile again.
On another occasion, Kongosi and the CRC team organized a
seminar in Bunia attended by about a hundred participants.
Afterwards, a man said to her, 'Yesterday, some people came to

ask me to contribute financially for war, but after this seminar I have decided that I can't support the war.'

Thirdly, in 2002, I received news that the Kinshasa Government's Minister for Human Rights, Ntumba Lwaba, would come to Bunia in the rebel-led district of Ituri. In the middle of his meeting with women's associations, the Minister asked their points of view. So Kongosi stood up and summarized briefly the true state of the political situation in the region. Her words were so powerful that the delegation from Kinshasa could not avoid crying. The Minister was so glad that he reacted by saying: 'You, women, you have strong power through your small voices. You can help your husbands, your sons and even other women by converting them for peace.' The same day, some women came and asked Kongosi what they could do for peace. As a result, a core group of women regardless of their ethnic origin was created and began working together for peace under the umbrella of the CRC. Some days later, UNOCHA (United Nations Office for the Coordination of Humanitarian Affairs) organized another meeting for women from different ethnic groups in conflict. These women hugged each other for the first time since the beginning of the war and agreed to work together for peace. Unfortunately, the situation deteriorated and the group collapsed.

Four steps ahead and ten steps back

We have seen these changes in individuals, but if people ask whether our peace work has brought about change in the whole situation, I have to say, 'Not yet.' People can feel terribly sorry for what they have done (often out of ignorance), but then new situations arise and the cycle of violence begins all over again. On 4 January 2001 for example, we did an evaluation as we did every year as Management Committee of the CRC. We were feeling very pleased because in the previous year we had done everything we had planned and the result was fantastically positive. Three days later, on 7 January 2001, the killings began again and we were so disappointed. In 2001, we had three clashes (in January, in August and in November) and thousands were killed. In 2002, there were ethnic clashes almost every month. As a result, since 1998, the Ituri district has lost 50,000 people and the Congo in general more than 3.5 million. Since September 2002, Nyankunde, this beautiful small town where we have been working for many years, was virtually deleted from the world map, like hundreds of other villages. This is the result of the civil war and occupation of the DRC, a war-game played in silence with the blessing of the West and the international community since 1998 and known as the 'First African World War'.[1]

Now, with the new crisis (May 2003), 80 per cent of the population of Bunia has fled and no one knows when they will come back, despite the presence of the multinational force. We were so discouraged. I'm reminded of the words of someone who came to help us from the US. He said: 'The work you are doing here is exactly the same as the work I am doing in the US, trying to help young people who have been taking drugs for a long time to stop. Many times we are discouraged. You can be working on a young person for four years and when you are sure that that young person is not taking drugs any more, you are so glad. But the very next day you hear he or she has begun taking drugs again. It's exactly like that in your case of conflict resolution and peace building.' So this is how I came to understand that peace building is a long process always going back to zero, a negative — to talk in mathematical language. The events actually bring you to a negative. Or in other words, you make four steps ahead and then, because of new events, you take ten steps back.

Part of the problem is that the Congo is very rich in minerals. In fact, it's like a man who is in trouble because he is married to a beautiful lady in the village. Everyone has eyes on that man and is plotting how to kill him. The beautiful lady in this case is the box of diamonds and uranium that everyone wants to get their hands on. The mineral dealers based in neighbouring countries Burundi, Rwanda and Uganda deliberately inflame the conflicts between local tribes and factions to give them a pretext for getting a foot in the country.

But we can't blame everything on outsiders. Congolese political leaders and young men have to be blamed also. Not long ago, we went to a UNESCO (United Nations Educational, Scientific and Cultural Organization) conference where we met intellectuals from Rwanda, Burundi and Uganda. The Congolese representatives were very angry with their colleagues from Rwanda because they were doing nothing to persuade their political leaders to stop the incursions into neighbouring Congo. Then a lady from Rwanda spoke — so powerfully that I will never forget it. She said, 'Do you think the Rwandans could get into the Congo without the complicity of the Congolese?' What she said is true. We have a lot of unemployed young men who can easily be bought into the militias. And even in our universities, leading academics can be manipulated and corrupted by promises of power and money from outsiders trying to get in. There is a saying, *'Mon diplôme a détruit le Congo'*. In other words, it is people with advanced degrees but no spiritual education who are destroying our country — selling it to the mineral dealers, for nothing.

This is why our work in peace education is so important. The people in power are already corrupted, so now we work with young people and children. I think of the African proverb: It's not easy to straighten a tree that has been bent by the wind for many years, but it is easy to do it to a small tree while it is still in the nursery. What we are trying to do is to give them spiritual power to produce strong leaders for the future — leaders whose power comes from their spiritual strength, not from the gun. These will be people who once in power will look for ways to provide for people's basic needs, and when there is conflict they will be able to call those in conflict together, sit round a table and discuss what is wrong. These are the kind of leaders we need and we are convinced that our training will bring them into being; we know that this is a long process, but this is what gives me hope. Those of us who are working in peace now will not see the results before we die, but the organization and the work will go on. I'm often discouraged, when I receive news about killings that are still going on in Ituri and the DRC in general, but the love of God keeps me going ahead.

To conclude, in CRC, we have three values that guide us: firstly love of God and of neighbour (because without God you can never love your neighbour as yourself), secondly tolerance, and thirdly nonviolence. These are our values.

Note

1 Mussanzi wa Mussangu, B., *First African World War, causes, effects and resolution, case of the Democratic Republic of Congo,* MA dissertation, Department of Peace Studies, University of Bradford, 2002.

Sima Simar

Sima Samar was born in 1957 in Ghazani, Afghanistan. She is a Hazara. Being a woman and from one of the most persecuted minorities she was very much at a disadvantage. Sima obtained a degree in medicine in 1982 from Kabul University. During the Russian invasion she joined the anti-Soviet resistance movement as a doctor. Following her husband's arrest in 1984 (he was never seen again), she and her son fled to Pakistan where she continued to practise medicine in a refugee camp in Quetta. With other women, Dr Samar established

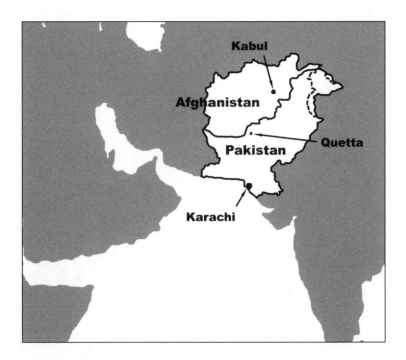

her first hospital for women in 1987. Two years later she set up the non-governmental Shuhada organization, whose focus is the reconstruction and development of Afghanistan, with special emphasis on women and children's empowerment. Since then the organization has been operating 12 clinics, 4 hospitals and 55 schools, both in Afghanistan and in refugee camps in Quetta. Sima was the Deputy Premier and Minister for Women's Affairs of the Interim Afghan Government (2001–2) and in 2002 became the Chair of the Independent Human Rights Commission. Sima received the Ramon Magsaysay Award in Community Leadership (1984) and the John Humphrey Freedom Award (2001).

I think the starting-point for my work was just the fact that I was born a female in this society where there is gross discrimination against women. I decided very early in my life to do something to change that society a little. That's why I started to fight with everyone — unfortunately — at home, at school and in the community. I was at school before the war and then, of course, after the invasion of Afghanistan, I was very much involved in activities against Russia.

I became a direct victim of the Russian invasion because I lost the husband I loved very much. He was a teacher in the university and he was taken from home one night for no reason, except that there was fighting in Kabul in which Shia were involved, and he was from a well-known Shia family. They picked up all the educated people that night — more than 500 in Kabul city, including my husband, and he never came back. Even now we are trying to find documents from that time — lists perhaps — which would tell us what happened to those people and how they were killed. Not only my husband, but also thousands of people were lost at that time.

As a woman and as a Hazara, I felt that things were really stacked against me, but I decided to continue the work I wanted to do. I started opening hospitals for women and children and setting up schools for girls, which was not easy (in fact it was really dangerous), but I believed that we could change society and people's attitudes through education. So that was my focus, and that is what I'm doing right now. I don't know whether the results are positive or negative but we are trying to bring about change.

In fact, there have been some positive changes. In one of the districts where I now have a lot of schools, there had been no schools for girls or hospitals catering adequately for women's needs. Now, we have enough nurses to help women with their problems and some of the girls from the schools are now at university. We have girls who have already become independent. They can stand on their own two feet and decide things for them-selves, which is a big change in our society. I think this is an important development because in those districts the whole attitude has changed. The authorities can no longer impose anything on the people.

Of course, it has been a struggle. In the late eighties, for example, it wasn't easy to deliver any kind of aid to Afghanistan. Every time I travelled, I had a lot of problems, both before the Taliban and during their rule. Supplies were looted by local people in some of the districts, but now nobody even talks negatively against our work so that's a big change. I was often tired and fed up with all the problems on the way and I would cry and say to myself that I would not come again. But after I had been in Pakistan for a few months, I would feel that I should go back to Afghanistan to see what was happening. So I would go through the same procedure all over again. I hope I can continue, but I'm getting older now and also my health is not that good. But I'll try to continue as long as I can.

At the moment, I'm Chairperson of the Independent Human Rights Commission which was established on 6 June 2002. We were not able to get an office until the following September when we hired this house. I bought a piece of carpet — I had to buy it at my own expense — and put it in one of the rooms and invited the commissioners to start work. We are now a bit more established because we finally got some money in our own hands in early February.

We are working in five fields of human rights. (I believe that without human rights we cannot have peace in this country.) The first is human rights education. I would like to educate the people about rights and of course responsibilities in order to help them to protect their own rights. The second is women's rights — we are trying to convince people that we are human beings and should be treated as human beings, not just as animals. It's not easy. It takes a lot of time to convince people. The third is children's rights. I believe the children are the future of the country and we have to enable them somehow to have a better education or a better environment to be good future citizens of this country. The fourth is work on 'transitional justice'. I believe we have to look at the past and do something about the past in order to bring justice and peace to this country. We really are trying to promote the idea of forgiveness, but we would like those people who committed the crimes at least to admit that they have done so and to ask for forgiveness from the people. They should not impose themselves as leaders through the power of the gun. The fifth is the monitoring and investigating of human rights abuses in my nation. We do receive a lot of complaints, and we do act on those cases that we are able to. We give information to the media. Sometimes I go and talk to the president myself, not just to change policy but also to give advice and recommendations on human rights issues.

This work is very demanding but I have had very heartening support from the public. The people really do want justice — this is the important thing. And one of the things which gives me personally the most encouragement is when people come and say that they really trust this commission because of my involvement in it.

Looking back, I can't say that this work has changed the direction of my life since I have been dealing with these issues for many years, but I am now working in a different capacity. I think there have been some positive achievements. I keep saying to myself that once I had 10,000 students and now I have 37,000. If out of the 37,000, 37 students become good and responsible citizens, then I have done what I wanted to do for the country. I'm also pleased about the hospitals that I established in very remote areas. If they have saved the life of one woman or a poor person who could not reach medical help otherwise, I feel happy.

These achievements give me a lot of satisfaction, but there has been a heavy price to pay at the personal level. I don't have the chance to enjoy family life. I lost almost everything. I have a son, but I don't see him often and we don't communicate very much. He is 25 and on his own now, but as a child he suffered because he was a victim of my actions. Once, he was locked in his home in Pakistan for three months because some people wanted to kidnap him. He was aware of all the suffering. I am thankful that he is strong, and grateful that he has supported my work. I also have a daughter of eleven who really does need me. She is in Pakistan because I don't trust the situation to bring her here and the quality of education is not that good. She has a better environment than my son — a better life actually. But she doesn't understand what it is I'm doing and keeps asking me to leave the job. She asks why I should keep working. I try to make her understand, but it's very difficult. My 77-year-old mother is in Pakistan too — and I am here so I don't see her very much. She's interested in what I'm doing and listens to the news because she wants to know what's happening in Kabul. Despite the difficulties, I am happy with the work I do. It may be only a drop in the ocean but at least if I am able to put one drop in the ocean it is something positive. I hope the people see me as a positive power because I trust the people more than any other kind of power.

I don't know what the future holds for me personally. I like to work with people at the grass-roots as I was doing before. Then I was Minister for Women's Affairs. It was not originally my choice to take on this human rights work, but I said to myself, 'OK, it's a challenge, and if I don't take it the women will be disappointed,' so I took the position and came here. Now I prefer this to my first job because I believe so strongly in the importance of human rights. But I don't know what the future will bring, because it's not only my decision. I think I still want to work with people, because the people do back my aims. Or maybe I will leave this work and practise my profession as a doctor, as I really enjoy helping people in need.

As for the future of Afghanistan, it's a country with a lot of problems. There are still gunmen around wielding power, and there's not much accountability in the country. The system isn't there yet. But I hope that we will be an institution that can help to bring in a sustainable peace and a more democratic system. I also hope we will have a lot of support from the international community because we cannot do it all on our own. That's the reality. We need outside pressure to support human rights rather than interventions to promote geo-political interests.

Douglas Sidialo

Douglas Sidialo was born in 1970 in Western province, Kenya. He married Teresa Odembo, a high school teacher, in 1996 and has two daughters, Sharon and Larvin. In 1995 he received his Diploma in Accounting from the Kenya College of Accountancy and for the following three years he worked as a marketing executive for Yamaha. He became blind as a result of the bombing of the American Embassy in

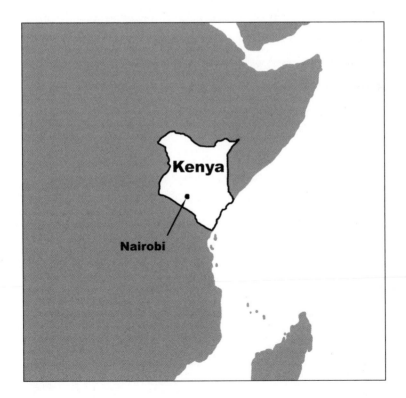

Nairobi on 7 August 1998. Since 1999, he has been the president of the Visual Seventh August, an organization formed by the victims of the bombing. He has been very active in networking with disaster victims and victims of terrorism, including those of the Oklahoma City bombing and their families, the Kenya Airways crash on the Ivory Coast, and September 11th.

I was born in Western province, Kenya, in 1970. There was nothing unusual about my life. Being brought up a Catholic, I have a deep Christian faith that was a major part of me even before my life was changed so abruptly. My education progressed into obtaining business-related qualifications, a Diploma in Accounting from the Kenya College of Accountancy and I also received computer training at the Kenya School of Professional Studies. In 1996 I married my wife Teresa, who is a high school teacher, and we now have two beautiful daughters. It was in 1995 that I obtained my job with Yamaha, East Africa, as a marketing executive in the overseas market dealing with the sale of motor-cycle products, outboard engines and water vehicles throughout East African countries.

The day on which my life and my family's lives were changed was 7 August 1998. On that day I was driving with a colleague in central Nairobi District. At the intersection of Haile Selassie and Moi Avenue I had stopped at the traffic lights. I noticed that a truck had made an illegal turn just before the intersection and entered the American Embassy compound. This unusual action caused a heated discussion between the truck driver and the

Kenyan security guards at the Embassy entrance. I heard what I thought were gunshots, which turned out to be exploding grenades, and my first thought was that somebody was carrying out a robbery at the Embassy. By this time the traffic lights had changed to green and I was close to the Embassy entrance. My last memory was of a man with a walkie-talkie radio running away from the sound of the grenades at the Embassy.

The next thing that I remember was hearing people wailing and crying close to and around me. This was three days later at the Kenyatta National Hospital in Nairobi, where I was told that there had been a terrible bomb blast at the Embassy and my colleague who was with me had been killed and my eyes were severely damaged. Unfortunately, despite the strenuous and skilful efforts of the doctors, it was not possible to save my eyes and I was to be blind for the remainder of my life. The realization that I would never see again was a terrible experience. Not only would I not be able to see my wife and children again, but as a registered blind person I would also lose my job. This was a devastating experience — my whole life changing in split seconds. I was in a state of shock, anguish, disbelief and anxiety, and initially I felt very bitter towards the people who had exploded the bomb, who turned out to be al-Qaida operatives.

Soon I realized that I would have to start learning all over again. My faith in God has been very significant to me and a bedrock in my healing and recovery process. In God and prayer I have derived the strength to soldier on with hope and courage; my faith in God gave me the hope to survive and the courage to confront all the trials that were placed before me. The rehabilitation training that I received covered adaptive technology, mobility, orientation and other necessary skills to give me some level of independence. It has not been easy for me to cope with being blind, having to rely on others for assistance and also wondering why some people in society are so evil that they are prepared to kill and maim innocent people.

My family, especially my wife Teresa, has given me enormous support both emotionally and socially throughout my rehabilitation process. Teresa has given me all as, being retired on medical grounds, I now depend on her for financial and material support. Also fellow victims of terror have helped a great deal by sharing experiences, in group therapy sessions, and this learning from others has been extremely valuable. Attending seminars and conferences on peace and trauma awareness has also helped my inner healing process.

The support that I have received has enabled me to move on and to help other victims, inspiring them on their journey of healing. Founding a support association for the survivors of the Kenyan bombing is part of this, providing mutual support and highlighting the plight of the survivors. I consider myself to be ecumenical, reaching out to all faiths and denominations with a message of peace. I have received amazing peace in my heart by forgiving those that have wronged me, those behind the Embassy bombing in Nairobi. The message of peace and reconciliation that I cherish and take every opportunity to speak about has had a profound effect on those who have heard it. People have left my talks changed in themselves and convinced of the importance of the message.

When the bombing happened in Oklahoma City this seemed a far-away occurrence; little did I know that three years later such a tragedy was too close to home and would cause the loss of my sight. With Oklahoma victims and survivors we've shown each other empathy, compassion and love so that we have become a family bound together by tragedy. Travelling to Oklahoma City in the year 2000 gave me much hope. Sharing experiences and reaching out to my American counterparts is really important as it enables survivors not to feel isolated in their anguish. If people feel that they are alone, then their trauma will never end. The Family foundation and contact that we have established between Kenyan and Oklahoma City victims is so solid and supportive and a great inspiration. After the tragic events at the World Trade Centre on 11 September 2001, I felt that it was especially important to reach out to the survivors and families there.

Attacks and atrocities such as those on the US embassies in East Africa, Oklahoma City and the World Trade Centre are evil and should not be allowed to happen again. It is all of our responsibilities to transform evil into good by promoting justice and peace all over the world. We should love our enemies and pray for them. It is a high order but worthy of the price.

Recently I have developed an immense passion for disabled sports, trekking thousands of miles on a tandem bicycle as a challenged athlete and hiking mountains to very high altitudes. Using sport as a tool, I deliver my message of peace and justice across the world and cry aloud to the powers that be to exercise caution, patience and restraint, and to seek effective and non-violent alternatives to war.

Bud Welch

Bud Welch has become an outspoken opponent of the death penalty, after coming to terms with the death of his daughter Julie in the Oklahoma City bombing. He has testified before the US Congress, many State Senate and House Judiciary Committees, made numerous radio and TV appearances, and met frequently with the father of Timothy McVeigh who was convicted of   planting the bomb. He is a member of Murder Victims Families for Reconciliation and serves on the Board of Directors of the Oklahoma City National Memorial Foundation.

I live in Oklahoma City in the United States. I'm an ordinary guy, a service station owner and farmer. As a family we have been in the area since my grandfather arrived in Oklahoma in 1892 during one of the last land rushes westward. He made a stand for what he felt was right by opposing the Ku Klux Klan who were prejudiced against a small number of Catholics in Oklahoma. Standing up for what we feel is right seems to run in the family.

We're a fairly close family. Every Wednesday I met my daughter, Julie-Marie, for lunch, we also talked on the phone a lot. In the eighth grade Julie met a non-English speaking Mexican girl who quickly became bilingual, and this made Julie long to speak a foreign language. She mastered Latin, German, Spanish and French. In high school she formed a chapter group for Amnesty International. She left Marquette University in 1994 and began work as an interpreter for the Social Security Administration in the Alfred P. Murrah Federal Building in Oklahoma City. Julie attended Mass each day at the Oklahoma City parish where Mexicans worship. She ran a children's programme. The children loved her. I wish I had her faith.

It was on Wednesday, April 19, 1995 that Timothy McVeigh left his truck containing a massive bomb opposite the Federal Building in Oklahoma City. This day changed my life and the lives of the families of 167 other people suddenly and tragically. That April morning, Julie had walked to the Social Security waiting room to meet a client when the bomb detonated. We were due to meet for lunch that day. On the morning of the bombing, one of my brothers telephoned just after 9.00 a.m. and told me to turn the television on. It showed the bomb damage at the Federal Building where Julie worked. I did not go to the bombsite; I would not have been allowed to get close. I waited for two days by the telephone, waiting for Julie's call; I hoped to hear her familiar voice. Instead I was told, on the Saturday after the bombing, that her body had been found. I was consumed by an almighty rage. I tried to numb the pain, but was obsessed with the idea of seeing the bombers die. I went to the site every day for a year; I was a physical and a mental wreck because I was stuck on April 19, 1995. All my life I opposed the death penalty, but the first four or five weeks after that bombing, after Tim McVeigh and Terry Nicholls (McVeigh's accomplice) had been arrested, I didn't even want a trial for them. I just wanted them to fry. That time is a blur; I just wanted McVeigh and Nicholls to be hanged, no trial being necessary. I could have killed them with my bare hands if I could have reached them.

Then, the realization dawned on me that trials were necessary. We didn't know beyond doubt that they were truly guilty. I asked myself, 'What is it going to do for me if McVeigh and Nicholls are executed?' I asked myself this question over and over but kept getting the same answer: their deaths would not help me one bit. It took me a full nine months to get to the point where I didn't want the death penalty for them. I remembered when Julie and I were driving in my car listening to a news radio station. They had told a story of yet another execution in Texas. Julie said, 'Dad, that makes me sick what they're doing in Texas. All they're doing is teaching hate to their children and it has no socially redeeming value.' I didn't think much about it at the time, but after Julie was killed it echoed in my mind every day. I now refuse to be a part of that hate. I finally realized that the death penalty was nothing more than revenge and hate — and revenge and hate are exactly why Julie and 167 others are dead. I still think of Julie every day but the need for retribution is out of my system. Execution is no solution. I wanted to ensure that Julie and the others had not died in vain; I wanted to talk to and persuade people that the death penalty is no answer.

In the first 72 hours after the bombing, President Bill Clinton and Attorney General Janet Reno promised to seek out, find the people responsible and apply the death penalty. At the time that was the big fix; my government was going to fix this horrible crime by causing more death. And I bought into that. I don't any more. I fear for our country. Our society should not tolerate a government with the power to kill its own citizens. It is wrong for the government to kill, no matter how heinous the crime. A person commits violence, and then our government compounds the violence.

We somehow believe that we can teach our children not to kill by killing. That is wrong. Americans must be made to understand that in Tim McVeigh's mind he was engaging in an act of revenge when he bombed a United States installation. In his mind he was at war. And much the same as when we bomb Iraq or send more than a billion dollars in weapons to Columbia, innocent civilians die and countless lives are changed forever. The 'collateral damage' from any war is the same: innocent people die. *We* must choose to stop the cycle of violence. To me the death penalty is vengeance, and vengeance doesn't really help anyone in the healing process. Of course, our first reaction is to strike back.

But if we permit ourselves to think through our feelings, we might get to a different place.

I spent a great deal of time travelling the country, urging that Timothy McVeigh should live. Julie would have wanted that. People listen to me. No one can say it hasn't happened to me, when I campaign against the use of the death penalty. In capital crimes where we impose the death penalty, society does not even think about the convicted person's family. But they are victims as well. I met Tim McVeigh's father William. I can't explain why, but since I met Bill McVeigh I feel closer to God. I'm not a real religious person, but that was an unforgettable experience. Bill McVeigh and myself have found the road to forgiveness and compassion difficult but possible to traverse.

The people who celebrated when McVeigh's sentence of death was announced surprised me. Vengeance solves no problems. The criminal commits a violent act. Then we, as a society, ratchet it up; we do him violence. Next we ask ourselves, 'Why are we such a violent society?' The execution of Tim McVeigh is not going to bring Julie or anybody else killed in the bombing back. And it's damn sure not going to bring me any peace. Reconciliation means accepting that you cannot undo the murder but you can decide how you want to live afterwards. After Timothy McVeigh was executed some people changed their minds about the death penalty because they realized that it hadn't helped them that he was not alive any more.

Most criticism of the death penalty focuses on how it affects the person on death row. My concern is how the death penalty affects the rest of society. Opposition to the death penalty is rooted in direct experience of loss and refusal to respond to that loss with a quest for more killing. Executions are not what will help us heal. We can all make a difference and together we must all work to end this cycle of violence. The Death Penalty Information Center collates the evidence: in 2001, the aggregated murder rate for all the US states with the death penalty was 5.82 murders per 100,000 people, whilst in the same period, in the states that do not have the death penalty, the murder rate was 4.25 per 100,000 people — and the rate has been consistently lower for at least the past ten years. I feel sure that I will continue with this work in my capacity on the board of Directors of Murder Victims' Families for Reconciliation.

> After a murder, victims' families face two things: a death and a crime. At these times, families need help to cope with their grief and loss, and support to heal their hearts and rebuild their lives. From experience, we know that revenge is not the answer. The answer lies in reducing violence, not causing more death. The answer lies in supporting those who grieve for their lost loved ones, not creating more grieving families. It is time we break the cycle of violence. To those who say society must take a life for a life, we say: 'not in our name'.

> Marie Deans, founder of Murder Victims' Families for Reconciliation

Terry Kay Rockefeller

Terry Kay Rockefeller attended The Johns Hopkins University and earned an MA in twentieth-century US history. She worked on documentaries, producing films on anthropology, science, history and politics. Among her credits is the history of the civil rights and black power movements, Eyes on the Prize. Most recently she executive-

produced a feature-length documentary on democracy in Africa. Terry's sister, Laura Rockefeller, was killed in the terrorist attacks on the World Trade Center. Since May 2002, Terry has worked with September Eleventh Families for Peaceful Tomorrows to honour her sister's life and to try to ensure that other families throughout the world do not experience the tragic and violent deaths of their innocent relatives. Rockefeller is a member of the Peaceful Tomorrows' board of directors. She speaks regularly about the need for nonviolent responses to terrorism and has travelled to Iraq as part of a citizen-to-citizen delegation to oppose US military action against that nation.

My sister, Laura, was a graduate of the musical theatre department at Syracuse University. Laura had a beautiful clear soprano voice and a warm, wonderful laugh. After she left Syracuse, Laura moved to Manhattan and dreamed of making her living in the theatre acting and singing. Sometimes she succeeded in getting the jobs she dreamed of — performing off-Broadway, touring with national theatre companies, directing and producing new plays. Other times she filled in with odd jobs to pay her bills and her rent.

On September 11, 2001, Laura left her upper-West Side Manhattan apartment at about 6 a.m. to report for a two-day stint on the 106th floor of the World Trade Center, helping to run a conference on risk assessment and information technology. When the job was over, Laura was planning to come to Massachusetts and visit us. But, of course, we never saw her again.

No one in our family knew that Laura was in the World Trade Center that day. It wasn't until late in the afternoon that one of her friends telephoned me because she feared the worst. After I confirmed with the company that had organized the conference that Laura had been there, I had to call my father and my mother and tell them their daughter was almost certainly dead. That is the hardest thing I have ever done in my life.

At first, I agonized over why Laura had to be at that job on that day. How had she ended up in the wrong place, at the wrong time? I felt that if I repeated the question often enough, it would somehow make it not be true. But, then I realized that this is the essential truth of all innocent victims of terrorism and war: they are in the wrong place at the wrong time.

When I think back to the weeks that followed September 11, one of my clearest memories is of the tremendous outpouring of support and compassion for those of us who were most directly affected by the terrorist attacks. It was evidenced in the large donations to charities to help victims' families. But there were smaller, personal gestures that meant just as much. Residents of Oklahoma City sent hundreds of teddy bears that had been left at the former site of the Murrah Federal Building to the Family Assistance Center in New York to let us know that we were not alone. A New York cabbie, who drove me to Pier 94, where I needed to go to file a missing person's report for Laura, refused to accept a fare from me. People appeared out of nowhere on the streets to offer you a cup of coffee, a bottle of water, or maybe just a hug. Those acts of kindness and connection helped me begin to heal.

One of the things I felt compelled to do when officials in New York allowed it was to visit the site of the World Trade Center. My parents who are in their 80s did not want to go. But my very dear friend — who coincidentally is also named Laura — said she would accompany me. It was an astonishingly beautiful day with bright sunshine and a brilliant blue sky. On the ferryboat ride down the Hudson River from the Family Assistance Center at Pier 94, a Navy chaplain who had been assigned to accompany Laura and me tried to determine what we were expecting to learn and experience. But there really was no way to prepare for the scene we encountered.

Thick smoke was rising from the remains of the twin towers. A landscape of twisted steel and concrete rubble stretched before us. My friend and I said very little to each other, but I remember clearly the first words I uttered, 'Someone wanted to do this.' It was a statement, not a question. I was overwhelmed by the intention of the violence of September 11. And that remains the most fundamental impression I have of that strange and difficult journey to Ground Zero.

I have described my visit to Ground Zero many times as I have spoken to community and college groups for September Eleventh Families for Peaceful Tomorrows. Very frequently I have been asked, 'Weren't you angry? Didn't you want revenge?' I always struggle with the answer. Yes I was angry, very angry that my sister —my only sibling — was taken from me, angry that I wouldn't hear her sing or laugh again. Angry that my parents' world had been devastated and that now I alone would care for them in their old age. Angry that Laura would not celebrate my daughters' school graduations, their weddings or the births of their children. Angry that Laura wouldn't fulfil a few more of her own dreams. Sometimes that anger left me sobbing in my rocking chair late at night. Other times it woke me, heart pounding, head throbbing in the pre-dawn hours. But revenge was a different matter.

Certainly knowing that the hijackers — those most directly responsible for Laura's death — were themselves dead contributed to my sense of the futility of seeking vengeance. Still, I knew the 19 hijackers were aided by others and I wanted (and continue to want) their accomplices to be identified, arrested, tried, convicted and incarcerated. Retaliatory violence, more killing in response to the unspeakable violence of 9/11 was, however, the last thing that made sense to me. And in this case the political became very personal: talk of war increased all my symptoms of post-traumatic stress syndrome. The thought of civilians dying in a far-off land made me feel that my sister was being killed yet again.

When bombs fell on Afghanistan, I had no idea if it would spell defeat for al-Qaida. I knew that it meant there would be thousands of families newly grieving, as mine already was. And my trip to Ground Zero had left me with a profound desire to work to ensure that nothing like it happened again. It was the compelling need I felt to act on that desire that led me to Peaceful Tomorrows. In January of 2002, I learned of four other 9/11 victims' relatives who had travelled to Afghanistan to meet with relatives of the civilians killed by our military action there. I wanted to be there with them. I knew in my heart that these brave travellers held a crucial key to how I would continue to heal.

Those four travellers, and a handful of other courageous indi-
viduals who had early and loudly opposed American war on
Afghanistan, organized Peaceful Tomorrows in February of 2002.
The organization takes its name from a speech by Dr Martin
Luther King, Jr in which he said:

> The past is prophetic in that it asserts loudly that wars are poor
> chisels for carving out peaceful tomorrows. One day we must come
> to see that peace is not merely a distant goal that we seek, but a means
> by which we arrive at that goal. We must pursue peaceful ends
> through peaceful means.

Seeking 'peaceful ends through peaceful means' is what compelled me to travel to Iraq in January of 2003. Deciding to go was
difficult and scary. I was definitely no supporter of Saddam
Hussein, indeed the entire time I was in Iraq I was deeply
distressed by my memory of America's support of his regime
during the 1980s — when Amnesty International and other
organizations were publicizing abundant evidence of his human
rights atrocities. When I was in Iraq, I was angry too that there
was no real opportunity for free dialogues with the civilians we
met. They lived in a climate of fear. We travelled with government
minders. And what we heard was a complex message to interpret.

Mostly the Iraqis were angry that their relatives — innocent
civilians — had died in the 1991 Gulf War and they feared yet
another round of killings. 'We do not hate Americans, but we do
not like your government,' they told us.

Sometimes, in quiet meetings, we simply grieved together
about our common pain. I remember especially the sincere
sympathy we received from a widow whose husband, a truck

driver, had been killed on December 1, 2002 — only six weeks before we met her — by a bomb dropped in the southern no-fly zone. We were welcomed into the circle of women who had joined her during the four months of mourning prescribed by Islamic tradition, and I will remember forever the tears she shed for us.

I will remember too the many Iraqis who told us they feared that war would lead to increased terrorism. American aggression and occupation of their lands by foreign troops would make it much easier to attract young men to the terrorist training camps, they warned us. And as I write this essay (in May of 2003), the 'jury is still out'. Did America 'liberate' Iraq, or are our troops now occupying Iraqi territory? Has war in Iraq made America and the world a safer place, or increased the threat of terrorism for people everywhere?

No one wants an end to terrorism more than I and the other members of Peaceful Tomorrows. But I believe the United States had taken a devastatingly wrong turn. We have squandered all the incredible compassion and support that was ours on September 12, 2001. Somehow, we need to return to that moment and rethink our actions. That has become the next piece of my chosen path to healing.

More and more I have found myself asking how I, as one victim of terrorism, might begin to envision a process of reconciliation with the people who espouse and even carry out terrorist acts. The work I imagine will be neither easy nor fast. It will require asking difficult questions, conducting careful research, and bravely confronting people who are doing wrong. We need to find out where the money that supports terrorism comes from and devise ways to halt its flow. The United States needs to join with other nations to create meaningful and effective courts of international law so that terrorists everywhere know there are standards of humanity and justice that they will be punished for violating.

But beyond finding out who harbours and supports terrorists, and working to make that impossible, I think we face an even greater challenge, which is to understand why people become terrorists. First, Americans need to recognize that there are reasons why people resent and hate us. We need to be willing to listen to them and learn from them, to acknowledge our mistakes and shortcomings, and to try to change. Secondly, we need to understand how and why potential terrorists choose their nihilistic path of violence. What is lacking in their societies that prevents them from seeing other options? What makes those who recruit people to a terrorist path so alluring? What can be done to diminish the allure of terrorism and offer constructive opportunities for people to improve their families' lives and the welfare of their nations?

And so I am trying to begin to think about how and where and with whom I — and other peacemakers — might be able to sit down together and talk about the root causes of terrorism. I am inspired by the Truth and Reconciliation Commission in South Africa, although I know it is only a partial model for what we need to achieve. Those who help lead the people of our world to do this urgent and difficult work can truly define the twenty-first century as a new era of global community.

September 11 was a defining moment for our world. We need to re-evaluate how our nation relates to the international community and we need to think about how, as Americans, we can help other nations change without seeking to control or dominate them. We must convince our leaders that the American public no longer sees war as a 'quick and easy' solution to the difficult and complex problems we confront.

Colleen Kelly

Colleen Kelly is the oldest of five children and grew up in Bucks County, Pennsylvania. Bill Kelly Jr, her younger and only brother, died in the World Trade Centre attack. She is a family nurse and one of the co-founders of the Ita Ford Health Team, a free clinic for uninsured people in East Harlem, New York. In early winter 2002, Colleen also contributed to the launch of September Eleventh Families for Peaceful Tomorrows for which she now works.

My name is Colleen Kelly. My brother, Bill Kelly Jr, was killed at the World Trade Center on September 11, 2001. He didn't work there. He just happened to be at a breakfast conference at Windows on the World. I have said all of this countless times, so much it almost makes me numb, as some type of self-preservation — except when I'm by myself, and not particularly thinking about Bill. Something might then happen to jolt my memory, usually unexpected. I think of him, and I cry.

I heard the most beautiful story yesterday. It affirmed my life's work these past 20 months. I belong to a group called the September Eleventh Families for Peaceful Tomorrows. We are a group of family members that all lost loved ones on September 11 who feel enough is enough. We don't want the death of almost three thousand people to be the rallying cry for more hurt, more violence, more heartache.

Peaceful Tomorrows has a two-part mission statement. The first is to seek out effective, nonviolent responses to terrorism. The second is to demonstrate a commonality with all people around the world affected by violence and terrorism. I suppose it's the second part of this mission that propelled Peaceful Tomorrows to send a delegation to Iraq in January 2003. We wanted to meet the ordinary Iraqi, the man or woman who had been experiencing years of state-sponsored violence, both from within and outside of Iraq. We didn't have to search too far. Almost everyone in Iraq has lost a loved one to war, sanctions or the cruelty of Saddam Hussein. This visit made me question deep down to the bottom of my soul the true meaning of good and evil. It had a profound effect — one I'm sure I still cannot fully grasp.

We were always under the watchful eye of a government minder. However, as a nurse and a mother, I like to think I know a little about human beings, regardless of the oppressive atmosphere. I can tell you that the Iraqis are an extremely hospitable people. I never felt threatened or unsafe. The Iraqis I met demonstrated enormous pride and resolve. As a people, it was clear they had suffered greatly. And with their suffering came strength, especially in the children. As a child, if you grow up with only hardship, then what do you know? How does that affect your future? Either you despair or you promise yourself to make a better life for your children, much like our grandparents and great-grandparents here in the States.

Well, a friend of mine, Kathy Kelly (no relation) has been concerned with issues surrounding Iraq for many, many years. She has visited Baghdad 19 times, and lived there for lengthy periods. She often hosts delegations to Iraq in her work as co-founder of Voices in the Wilderness. And one of the places she has repeatedly visited with these different delegations is the paediatric oncology units of Iraqi hospitals. There is growing support for the theory that the use of depleted uranium during the first Gulf War has contributed to the three-or-fourfold increase in childhood cancers in Iraq. What we know for sure is that kids with cancer can't get their chemotherapy as scheduled (or at all) because of sanctions. We also know for fact that the studies that should have been done to monitor the rise in oncologic illness never were. Kathy felt at one point she needed to see healthy kids too, as she was beginning to lose perspective on the life of an average Iraqi child. She asked her minder to take her to a place full of children who weren't so sick, and she was escorted to the Baghdad School of Music. Once there, she was given a tour, including a look at much of the children's recent artwork. She happened to notice a picture of what looked like the World Trade Center and a plane about to crash into it. So Kathy asked the kids, 'Who drew the picture?' and could she talk to him or her.

Within minutes, the artist was brought forth. Kathy asked him, 'What were you thinking when you drew this picture?' His reply, in halted English, was this: 'I do this so America know what it like when America do this to others.' When I heard Kathy recall this I felt so angry and hurt. I thought of Bill and defensively surmised what a stupid and horrible thing for this boy to say. But there's more to this story.

Kathy went on to explain to the young artist all about Peaceful Tomorrows. How there were relatives of people killed in that very picture that didn't want him, or his family, or anyone else to be hurt. She told him how these family members travel all over speaking about their loss, and how they don't want this to happen to anyone else. She made it clear to all the children that there were people who thought there must be another way, that we didn't have to keep doing this to others. The director asked Kathy if she had a favourite song, one she might like to teach the children. Kathy then sang *Finlandia,* in both English and her limited Arabic. When Kathy returned to the school three days later, the children surprised her with a rendition of Finlandia they had been diligently practising.

I'm not sure what to make of this story except it makes me glad. Glad that September Eleventh Families for Peaceful

Tomorrows exists. Glad that Kathy was in Baghdad. Glad that this boy, the young artist, heard of our loss, and most importantly, our response. I think of the possibility of ever meeting this boy when he's older, a young man. I don't know if this chance meeting with Kathy will ever change how he thinks or feels. But somehow, I feel much safer knowing it happened.

This scenario made me re-think the repercussions of September 11. I have felt to the core of my being that nonviolent justice was the only possible response to this tragedy. But now I want to expand that argument. Not only does my heart tell me this but now my brain as well.

I do not feel any safer in this world today than I did in the fall of 2001. Does anyone? Bombings in Bali and Casablanca. War in Afghanistan and Iraq. Children shooting children. Detained nameless and faceless prisoners. Chronic 'orange alert'. I think a lot about the most effective means of apprehending those responsible for the crimes of September 11. To date, the most senior members of al-Qaida to be captured have been caught because of good intelligence, not military conflict. I feel it's wrong to wage wars where the majority of the dead and wounded are non-combatants. I think the focus of pre-empting the manifestations of terrorism is good, but looking at the root causes — what makes a human lose so much of their connectedness to humanity that they are willing to kill themselves and thousands of others — is better.

I feel Bill is OK.

I know my brother wasn't killed by a weapon of mass destruction, but by a $4.99 box cutter. I feel the real weapon of mass destruction is someone's *mindset*, whether a dispossessed, fanatical man or one that's prestigious, powerful and recognized. Both can act recklessly. I know the world has the energy, imagination and resources to choose to tackle this problem.

With all that we think and feel, we have a choice. We (all of us) can set children loose into the world with memories of violence and destruction. Or we can become teachers, storytellers, and examples of an alternative. I want to meet that child from Baghdad, the young artist, knowing he's heard the story of the hope for a peaceful tomorrow.

Finlandia by Jean Sibelius:

This is my song, O God of all the nations. A song of peace for lands afar and mine. This is my home, the country where my heart is. Here are my hopes, my dreams, my holy shrine. But other hearts in other lands are beating, with hopes and dreams as true and high as mine. My country's skies are bluer than the ocean, and sunlight beams on cloverleaf and pine. But other lands have sunlight too, and clover, and skies are everywhere as blue as mine. O hear my song, thou God of all the nations. A song of peace for their land and for mine.

Robert Green

Commander Robert Green served in the British Royal Navy from 1962 to 1982, where his work was involved with the Ministry of Defence's nuclear weapons capability. After his voluntary redundancy in 1982, and after the unsolved murder of his aunt Hilda Murrell, an anti-nuclear campaigner, he began to examine and then challenge the hazards of nuclear electricity generation. He now lives in Christchurch, New Zealand (NZ), where he and his wife Dr Kate Dewes have established the Disarmament and Security Centre as a branch of the NZ Peace Foundation. They are working closely with the NZ Government on disarmament issues.

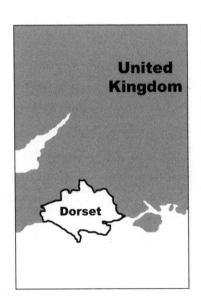

My sudden decision, aged 8, to join the Royal Navy (RN) understandably caused my parents puzzled surprise. My father was a middle-ranking expert on farm building design in the Ministry of Agriculture, having lectured before and after World War II at London University's Agricultural College in Wye, Kent, where I was born in 1944. I recently discovered that in 1952 a cousin of my father was serving as a Commander RN, but had lost touch with him. In World War II, my father had been a War Department Land Agent with acting rank of Captain in the Grenadier Guards, negotiating compensation for farmers whose land had been commandeered. That was the sum total of my   military connections!

When I decided on a career as a naval officer, I was on holiday with my family in a Cornish fishing village. Warships were often faintly visible on the horizon near Devonport naval base, and I fell in love with boats and the sea. The Coronation Fleet Review at Spithead the following summer redoubled my innocent enthusiasm. On repeating the Cornish holiday that August, I badgered my father into arranging for me to visit a warship, an elegant old cruiser *HMS Euralyus,* in Devonport. The second-in-command (a Commander) personally welcomed me aboard the quarterdeck like royalty. I was dazzled, and never considered any other career.

Being very conventionally middle class, joining meant going for officer. My parents took good advice and sent me to the Nautical College, Pangbourne — now a minor 'public' (private fee-paying) boys' school called Pangbourne College, between Reading and Oxford in Berkshire. The spartan routine and harsh discipline were a shock, but from age 13 I weathered the daily early morning run followed by cold hosing down, corporal punishment and endless parades in the uniform of Cadet, Royal Naval Reserve. It was a junior replica of the Britannia Royal Naval College Dartmouth, which made the transition into the Navy effortless.

On joining Dartmouth direct from school in 1962, I discovered I was unusual in having no military pedigree. This meant that I had a relatively detached and enquiring attitude to naval life and traditions. The warships did not disappoint me; I relished my sea time, and was surprised and encouraged to find the Navy seemed to like me when I was awarded a Queen's Telescope as one of the five top Cadets in my first year.

Towards the end of my second year as a Midshipman gaining sea experience in Malta, my mother committed suicide. A manic-depressive, she had also struggled with breast cancer. Her death fired me with a single-minded drive to fulfil her desire for me to succeed in my chosen profession. I went on to achieve a first-class pass from naval training, which put me in the fast lane for promotion to Commander.

Two years later, I found myself press-ganged into the Fleet Air Arm as an Observer, the naval equivalent of navigator. The Admiralty needed to fill vacancies caused by an alarming increase in fatal accidents among jet aircrew. Again to my surprise, I found that I enjoyed it, and passed out top of my course. This meant that I was assigned to one of the Navy's elite squadrons, flying in Buccaneer nuclear strike jets with a target in Russia.

After my mother died, her elder sister Hilda Murrell filled the void. Despite my youth and inferior education, Hilda and I 'clicked'; she became my mentor and a close friend. A former Cambridge English graduate who also showed considerable flair in business and as a plantswoman, she successfully ran the family rose nursery in Shrewsbury, Shropshire from 1949 to 1970. She had an infectious enthusiasm for all forms of life and their miraculous harmony on this beautiful but fragile planet. She particularly loved the British Isles, their long history and how it had shaped the landscape, architecture and, of course, the gardens. Yet she was seldom nostalgic. On the contrary, she constantly probed the future, always with an eye to protecting humanity's cultural heritage and increasingly polluted environment.

Having predicted the 1973 oil crisis five years before, she told me: 'The next will be nuclear.' She did her homework, and homed in on the nuclear energy industry's financial profligacy and failure to solve the waste problem.

Meanwhile, I was flying nuclear weapons around in strike jets and then anti-submarine helicopters. I rationalized (wrongly) that it was possible to support the Bomb and Hilda's views on nuclear energy. This was fortunate when I was promoted to Commander in 1978, and sent to the Ministry of Defence as personal staff officer to an Admiral closely involved in recommending the replacement for the Polaris nuclear-armed ballistic missile submarine force.

I watched the powerful nuclear submarine lobby — known in the Navy as the 'black mafia' — go ruthlessly for a scaled-down version of the huge US Trident submarine system, even though it grossly exceeded UK requirements, introduced a destabilizing first-strike capability with its greater firepower and accuracy, and its massive cost threatened the future of the Royal Navy as a balanced, useful force.

Margaret Thatcher became Prime Minister during this time. Addicted to all things nuclear, she forced the British nuclear energy industry to accept the US pressurized water reactor design that had just failed so spectacularly at Three Mile Island. She welcomed the stationing of US nuclear-armed Cruise missiles on British soil, in the face of huge public protest. And she decided to have Trident without consulting her Cabinet. Despite misgivings, the Chiefs of Staff were brought into line.

My main reason for applying for redundancy in the Thatcher government's 1981 defence review was that, having been pro-moted to Commander very early after a career spent almost exclusively in aviation, I was ill-equipped to succeed in the fierce competition to command a frigate, without which I would not reach the rank of Admiral. Underlying this, however, was my concern that I could not stay fully committed to the Navy if it had to operate Trident.

On leaving the Navy after 20 years at the end of 1982 aged 38, with a working wife and no children, I trained as a roof thatcher in Dorset where we were living. Enduring many bad puns from friends about the political regime, I thatched for eight idyllic years. This proved vitally therapeutic following Hilda's bizarre, high profile murder. At the time of her death, Hilda was 78 years old. After retiring, her passion for preserving the British country-side had led her to campaign against both nuclear energy and weapons. She correctly saw radioactive waste as the Achilles heel of the nuclear industry, and that nuclear electricity generation in its current form was unsafe and could not be sustained without massive government subsidies.

On 21 March 1984, she was preparing to testify as an independent objector on radioactive waste management problems at the first public inquiry into a nuclear power plant in Britain, at Sizewell in Suffolk. At about midday, following a break-in at her home when only a little cash was found to be missing, she was apparently abducted in her own car, which was seen being driven erratically by several witnesses. It was quickly reported abandoned on the side of a lane just outside Shrewsbury; but her mutilated body was not found for three days, in a wood half a mile across fields from the car. Despite one of the biggest police investigations in Britain in the twentieth century, the case remains unsolved.

While pursuing the truth about her murder, I took up Hilda's baton campaigning against the hazards of nuclear-powered electricity generation, especially after the first nuclear explosion in a power plant at Chernobyl in April 1986. The British nuclear energy industry had begun as a cynical by-product of the race to provide plutonium for nuclear weapons. Furthermore, the US-UK nuclear lobby is extremely powerful, secretive and ruthless. Nevertheless, for as long as possible I steered clear of being drawn into the ultimate step of opposing 'the Bomb'.

This happened in January 1991, just before the US-led coalition began its air bombardment of Iraq in the first Gulf War. My military intelligence training had warned me that Saddam Hussein would be given the pretext he needed to attack Israel, in order to split the coalition and become the Arabs' champion. If provoked enough, he could use Scud ballistic missiles with chemical or biological warheads. If such an attack caused heavy Israeli casualties, Israel's Prime Minister Shamir would come under massive domestic pressure to retaliate with a nuclear strike on Baghdad. Even if Saddam Hussein did not survive (he had the best anti-nuclear bunkers that Western technology could provide), the entire Arab world would erupt in fury against Israel and its allies; its security would be destroyed forever; and Russia would be sucked in.

The first Scud attack hit Tel Aviv on the night of 17 January 1991, two days after the Allied *blitzkrieg* began. A week before I had addressed a crowd of 20,000 anti-Gulf War demonstrators from the foot of Nelson's column in Trafalgar Square of all places. In so doing, I became the first ex-British Navy Commander with experience of operating nuclear weapons to have come out against them. In Israel, for the first time, the second city of a *de facto* nuclear state had been attacked and its capital threatened. Worse for nuclear deterrence dogma, the aggressor did not have nuclear weapons. The Israeli people, cowering in gas masks in basements, learned that night that their so-called 'deterrent' had failed in its primary purpose. Some 38 more Scud attacks followed.

Seymour Hersh, in his bestseller *The Samson Option,* recounts how Israel reacted:

The [US] satellite saw that Shamir had responded to the Scud barrage by ordering mobile missile launchers armed with nuclear weapons moved into the open and deployed facing Iraq, ready to launch on command. American intelligence picked up other signs indicating that Israel had gone on a full-scale nuclear alert that would remain in effect for weeks. No one in the Bush administration knew what Israel would do if a Scud armed with nerve gas struck a crowded apartment building, killing thousands. All Bush could offer Shamir, besides money and more batteries of Patriot missiles, was American assurance that the Iraqi Scud launcher sites would be made a priority target of the air war. Such guarantees meant little; no Jews had been killed by poison gas since Treblinka and Auschwitz, and Israel, after all, had built its bomb so it would never have to depend on the good will of others when the lives of Jews were being threatened. The escalation didn't happen, however; the conventionally armed Scud warheads caused — amazingly — minimal casualties, and military and financial commitments from the Bush administration rolled in. The government of Prime Minister Yitzhak Shamir received international plaudits for its restraint. American officials were full of private assurances for months after the crisis that things had been under control; newsmen were told that Israel, recognizing the enormous consequence of a nuclear strike, would not have launched its missiles at Baghdad. The fact is, of course, that no one in America — not even its President — could have dissuaded Shamir and his advisers from ordering any military actions they deemed essential to the protection of their nation.

Meanwhile, in Britain, the Irish Republican Army just missed wiping out the entire Gulf War Cabinet with a mortar bomb attack from a van in central London. A more direct threat to the government could barely be imagined. What if instead they had threatened to use even a crude nuclear device? A counter-threat of nuclear retaliation would have been utterly incredible.

Belatedly forced to research the history of 'the Bomb', I discovered that the British scientific-politico-military establishment bore considerable responsibility for initiating and spreading the nuclear arms race. Having alerted the US to the feasibility of making a nuclear weapon, the UK participated in the Manhattan Project. On being frozen out of further collaboration, in 1947 the UK began to develop its own nuclear arsenal. The UK became Saddam Hussein's role model: the first medium-sized power with delusions of grandeur to threaten nuclear terrorism. Also the doctrine of nuclear deterrence had always been flawed in terms of its practicality, and was immoral and unlawful; and there were more credible and acceptable alternative security strategies.

Having given up thatching as the Gulf War loomed, later in 1991 I became Chair of the UK affiliate of the World Court Project. This worldwide network of citizen groups helped to persuade the UN General Assembly, despite desperate counter-moves led by the three NATO (North Atlantic Treaty Organization) nuclear weapon states, to ask the International Court of Justice (known as the World Court) for its Advisory Opinion on the legal status of nuclear weapons. In 1996, the Court confirmed that the threat, let alone use, of nuclear weapons would generally be illegal. For the first time, the legality of nuclear deterrence had been challenged. Also, I met Kate Dewes, a pioneer of the project living in Christchurch, New Zealand, and we both became members of the project's International Steering Committee from 1992 to 1996. After we were married in 1997, we established a Disarmament & Security Centre in the South Island branch of the Peace Foundation, which she had coordinated from her home for over 20 years.

There is no doubt in my mind that the two traumas involving the violent deaths of my mother and then her sister were pivotal in my conversion from operator of nuclear weapons to campaigner for their abolition. My mother's death steeled me and lifted me to excel as an Observer, without which I would not have had the experience of operating nuclear weapons. The pursuit of the truth about my aunt's murder forced me to learn about how the nuclear industry and successive governments had corrupted and abused British democracy and the Royal Navy.

The extreme and unique nature of my family experiences may help to explain why I remain the only ex-British Navy Commander with nuclear weapon experience to have come out against them. I also attribute a major influence to the peculiarly potent tradition, carefully nurtured to carve out and hold down the British Empire, immortalized by Tennyson in his Crimean War poem *The Charge of the Light Brigade* about an earlier suicide mission. The attitude 'Theirs not to reason why, theirs but to do and die' was alive and well, especially in the all-volunteer Royal Navy.

However, my father set a fine example as a truly gentle man who did not pressure me in any way to follow any macho tendencies (though I had plenty of that in the Navy!). My first wife was a major factor in my early promotion to Commander, and my rock in the massive shift from naval life to self-employed artisan. In my final transformation to peace activist, I would not have been able to do that without the support base provided by Kate.

My naval career gave me first-hand experience of operating nuclear weapons. As the first British ex-Commander with that experience to have spoken out against them, this has proved to be a unique qualification. Of almost equal importance, I received an excellent training to communicate this.

My specialization of Observer seems curiously apt to describe my whole naval experience. With no military pedigree, I went through it subconsciously treating the Navy rather like an anthropologist who 'goes native' with a tribe in order to study them. That said, the decision to take redundancy was traumatic, as I had no other qualifications and had been sheltered from the real world outside the military.

Thereafter, I feel I have been swept along in a process of responding to huge events. These include Hilda's murder, Chernobyl, the end of the Cold War, the first Gulf War, being elected UK Chair of the World Court Project, divorce in 1992, re-marriage in 1997, and my father's death followed by emigration to New Zealand in 1999.

With all these, I made conscious choices. However, I have a sense of following a definite path for which my experiences seem to have prepared me.

My life has been blessed, guided and changed by a succession of strong women: my mother Betty, her sister Hilda, my first wife Liz, and now Kate. My father Noel was there for me in quiet support until recently. After I 'jumped off the cliff' before the first Gulf War and joined the anti-nuclear movement, one of my inspirations was Admiral of the Fleet Earl Mountbatten of Burma, whose last speech against nuclear weapons in May 1979 probably cost him his life three months later — though the cover story was that the IRA (Irish Republican Army) bombed his yacht. Among sudden new mentors were Air Commodore Alastair Mackie, Peter Smith, Brigadier Michael Harbottle and Frank Barnaby of

Just Defence, Paul Rogers, Bruce Kent, Frank Blackaby, Scilla Elworthy and Joseph Rotblat.

In listing the above, I must emphasize that my trauma at speaking out against nuclear weapons was heightened by my fear of being branded as an emotional CND (Campaign for Nuclear Disarmament) supporter. Apart from having been in an extremely sensitive Navy appointment when the first Thatcher government began to persecute CND, I knew that Hilda had not joined CND. She carefully chose the Nuclear Freeze movement and END — although she had quietly supported the Greenham women and attended the November 1983 CND rally in London. Like her, I saw CND's approach as too emotional, too pacifist, and alienating the Establishment. I, too, realized that I must not sever my Establishment connections, but rather try to turn them to good use. That is why initially I only joined Ex-Services CND and Just Defence.

Just Defence was important to me because it offered an alternative defence and security paradigm, without which any attempt to get rid of nuclear weapons would founder. Building on the work of the Palme Commission that security needed to be transformed from a win/lose military game to a safety net for all, Just Defence upheld the UN and advocated the OSCE (Organization for Security and Cooperation in Europe) instead of NATO, and promoted preventive diplomacy, minimal non-provocative defence and conversion of the arms industry to peaceful uses.

My own research into the history of Britain's nuclear weapons and policy led me to single out two aspects on which to focus my energies: the law, and nuclear deterrence. These related closely to my military experience, and especially to the principal difference between military professionals and hired killers or terrorists: military professionals must be seen to act within the law.

Challenging the legality of nuclear weapons brought me into the World Court Project as the British chair of this remarkably successful and innovative international campaign, one of whose pioneers from Christchurch, New Zealand, was Kate. I was in the audience when she stole the show at the international launch of the campaign in Geneva in May 1992. Our relationship blossomed after we were appointed as members of the International Steering Committee. Although I spent most of my time in the UK between then and the World Court's verdict in 1996, I was enormously motivated and sustained by our teamwork from opposite sides of the planet, with frequent meetings in New York and Europe.

After the World Court confirmed that the threat or use of nuclear weapons would generally be unlawful, my work shifted to promoting the Court's advisory opinion and campaigning to per-suade the nuclear powers to comply. Two new mentors emerged following publication of the report by the Canberra Commission on the Elimination of Nuclear Weapons in August 1996. The first, a member of the Commission, was recently retired General Lee Butler, USAF, while the other was the Commission's consultant on nuclear deterrence, Michael MccGwire. Lee is my generation, and his last job had been as Commander-in-Chief of Strategic Command, in charge of all US nuclear forces from 1992 to 1994. In December 1996, he decided to speak out against nuclear weapons, and was the most eloquent and authoritative advocate yet. When he came to New Zealand in October 1997, Kate and I were able to spend several hours with him and his wife, and they gave us huge affirmation and encouragement.

Mike MccGwire and I had both left the Royal Navy prematurely as Commanders after working in naval intelligence. In the 1960s and 70s, he revolutionized the analysis of Soviet naval strategy both in the UK and US. He went on to challenge the established view of nuclear deterrence, and was unusually effective because of his deep expertise on Soviet military thinking. Although his approach was academic, he provided intellectual underpinning for my arguments, and was wonderfully encouraging as a former British naval colleague.

Between them all, my mentors inspired me to write down my findings and hone my arguments. This was the principal resource which I discovered, and on which I am now focusing my work.

My life so far has borne out the saying, beloved of Hilda: 'To struggle and to understand — never one without the other.' My metamorphosis from nuclear warrior to peace activist has taught me that the only durable security is as a safety net for all, not a 'win/lose' military game. Indeed, the nature of modern warfare is such that, not only do non-combatants make up over 90 per cent of the casualties, but even the 'victorious' military are suffering long-term health effects, probably from inoculations against chemical or biological weapons and/or use of toxic materials such as depleted uranium. Besides, the many threats to our security are increasingly seen to be beyond solution by military means. Overarching my work is an urgent need to reclaim patriotism in a new form embracing the whole earth, before narrow nationalism destroys us all.

Rachael Burgess

Rachael Burgess was born in 1965, and after a conventional but musically oriented education in Nottingham she turned down a place at university. Instead she was commissioned into the Royal Air Force (RAF), serving in the UK and abroad, seeing operational service in Bahrain and Kuwait, northern Iraq during the first Gulf War, and on peace support operations in the Balkans. She values enormously the experiences she gained in a military career spanning 13 years. After her resignation, marriage and motherhood, she now divides her time

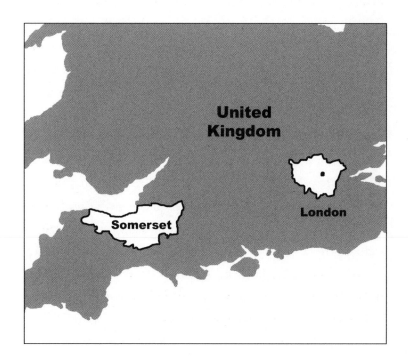

between her passions which are her family, and researching and writing about innovative approaches to resolving conflict — from the personal to the global level. As well as contributing directly, she was also involved in Unarmed Heroes *as a member of the editorial team.*

I am often asked how I transformed my career from being in the Royal Air Force to being part of the editorial team that has helped to produce this book. At the age of 20, in 1986, when I walked through the doors of the Royal Air Force College at Cranwell to begin my Initial Officer Training, I believed that I would be contributing to world peace by preparing to defend my country. At the age of 38, in 2003 as I write this account, what has changed? Nothing and everything. Nothing, in that I still believe that I am contributing to world peace, and everything in that this time it is world peace instead of world aggression. In the past, partly because of my youthful ignorance and naivety, I surrendered my life to the military to be used for what I now know to be, with the benefit of hindsight, the pursuit of political ends. Together with a growing band of people, I use my life to seek credible ways for civilians to resolve conflict on every level from personal to global.

The deep sense of purpose that once guided me to join the RAF is moving steadily from a position of powerlessness to one of joy and a desire to be of service to myself and to others. The transition is as much about being a daughter, wife, mother and friend as it has been about changing my professional contribution to humanity from military to civilian methods.

So what led me to choose the RAF back in the mid-eighties? I had gained a place at university to read music with a view to working in a recording studio and was confronted with the insecurity that surrounded the music industry. In contrast, the RAF promised a well-mapped career that would develop me into a confident and well-travelled individual, and indeed in many ways I had a fantastic career. I can't imagine another job available at the time that would have enabled me to travel to so many amazing places and work with so many fascinating people. I look forward to discovering a civilian organization that offers as much.

On reflection I am intrigued as to how I managed to survive in such a male dominated environment for 13 years. Choosing a career in a man's world was one of the steps to becoming out-wardly 'one of the boys'. Inwardly, however, I must have already had the characteristics that enabled me to survive as long as I did. In the military there was little room for the emotions. Driven by my perception that I was required to strive at all times for a stan-dard of so-called 'appropriate' behaviour that was beyond criticism, my military training reinforced a need to suppress my emotional feelings. After all, the training led me to prepare for a time when it could be 'appropriate' for me to shoot someone. Emotional and indeed spiritual guidance were catered for during training by a couple of lectures where the chaplains made their availability known. During war I found few atheists, and maybe if I had taken up the padres' offer of support during peacetime my life would have been easier.

I refused to acknowledge any form of emotional difficulty and would happily trot out the military mantra about 'getting on with the job I'd been trained to do'. My fear of letting myself be out of control turned into a fear of failure. As the fears piled up my original vocation to be a force for the good crumbled into a state of anxiety and self-doubt.

My unhappiness was due at least in part to the undercurrents of intolerance and prejudice, and to the many unhappy battles, personal and professional, individual and collective, that were going on around me. Seven years after I had served in the 1991 Gulf War, and six years after being in Croatia, I realized that the only war I was still fighting was my own. Ignorance and the denial of the stress I was under led to a constant base level of discontent and eventually to the point that my physical health was suffering.

My days consisted of driving to work, being at work, getting home again and sleeping. Increasingly I was making appointments with the doctor for seemingly random complaints. I felt as though my uniform no longer fitted and that something had to give. The 'system' was bigger than me and I finally recognized my need to sever my commitment to the RAF despite the financial implications of leaving before the end of my commission.

I resigned in July 1998, my last day of service was in February 1999, and a very angry me was catapulted into the sea of civilian unknown. Despite having a supportive partner, David, insecurity reigned as I stripped away the structure that had been my life. I had been trained in a particular leadership mould containing power and influence and soon realized that the only person I could directly influence and had the power to change was myself.

I lost count of the avenues I considered where I might usefully be employed, from the defence industry to complementary medical practice. At the same time I was challenging my inner self by exploring various spiritual paths, from Christianity to the occult. I had no reference points to use as anchors as I grappled with this identity crisis, and it became hard to understand and relate to others or myself. Sometimes it still feels that way, although now I have more inner resources to call on. Four years ago such freedom deleted was as destabilizing as my confinement within the military; this confinement experienced at the end of my career was the *security* I had felt at the beginning.

Some eight months into being a civilian I came across Scilla Elworthy's work, and a new direction began to emerge. In the autumn of 1999 I read two of her articles that led me to her book *Power and Sex* and to attend the Bristol Schumacher Lectures on 'Rethinking Security' where she presented 'Dealing with Bullies Without Using Bullets'. I nervously introduced myself, tentatively offering my help for anything that might be useful. However, soon I was forced to conclude that it was my own inner work that needed attention now, before I could be useful in an outer sense.

I knew I had to take a very personal first step in understanding if and how the military training and environment had led me to think more like a man than a woman. Was there a gentle strength within me rather than the bully? If so, how could I find it? These were questions that only I could answer by challenging things I had previously held dear. My pride was one of them. I read in horror the following passage in *Power and Sex* written by Squadron Leader Jones from the Royal United Services Institute:

We live today, at the end of the 20th century, in a world increasingly polarized, between light and dark, between haves and have-nots, between us and them, between men and women. War seduces us in part because we continue to locate ourselves inside its prototypical emblems and identities. Men fight as symbols of a nation's sanctioned violence. Women work and weep and sometimes protest, but traditionally always as the collective 'other' to the male.[1]

There I was, a *woman* who had fought as a symbol of a nation's sanctioned violence and here was a man describing women who '… *work and weep and sometimes protest … as the collective "other" to the male'*.

He went on to describe women in the armed forces thus:

… many become so immersed in their male identity that women became 'the other' in their eyes; in the military they became 'one of the boys'. Often the only way for women to cope with the contradiction of being both a female and a soldier was actively to deny their connection with the feminine world. To expect such female warriors to challenge an institution in which they held such a precarious position was unrealistic.

Although I was shocked and part of me wanted to dismiss his opinion as rubbish, I decided to resolve just how accurate this man's opinion was where I was concerned. Had I become so removed, quote marks immersed, in my male identity that women had become 'the other' in my eyes? As I cast my mind back over my career it seems obvious now that the only way to survive in such a man's world was to become 'one of the boys' which then resulted in women becoming 'the other'.

Often, being the only woman around, I had begun carelessly to accept the male way of talking about women, believing the refrain

'If you can't take it, you shouldn't have joined'. I had developed my own form of defensive retorts that acted as a personal boundary. Successful as my retorts were in male company, they were absolutely useless when faced with a bunch of female US Army soldiers with whom I shared a tent on the edge of an airfield in northern Iraq. Listening to them one evening I discovered what going beyond being 'one of the boys' was about. I felt so threatened that I retreated back into the relative safety of the man's world.

It was five years before I once again realized that I didn't fit in with the women around me. I had been posted to the Royal Air Force Staff College in Bracknell where families were accommodated on the base. During an informal social event in the back garden of a married quarter, I was faced with a dozen or so women, the service wives. I had nothing in common with them. They were busy trying to run homes, families and various types of civilian jobs — things about which I was truly ignorant. They were not interested in the details of their husband's actual employment, the individual business of war. After all, why should they want to understand? Who would want their daughters to do what I was doing? I had to face the stark contrast between us, the female service personnel, and them, the service wives. And if I wanted to do anything about it, I had to see it as my problem not theirs. I needed some of them to wake up and acknowledge their part because the fact that they couldn't afford to think let alone talk about the consequences of their husbands' actions was scaring me. I wanted to shout, but my anger would have got in the way of what I wanted anyone to hear. All I wanted was a civilian woman to listen to the hurt that I was feeling inside, because to me military men were powerless. I saw their faces as blank silence. This was a silence that deafened me with trivia for a few more years before I realized that I really needed to learn to listen to myself, and before that I had to look after my own anger. Resolving the issues raised for me as a woman by my years in the service has involved wading through many deep levels of pain, fear, anger and disconnection.

Leaving the RAF did not mean I had finished struggling with institutions, including the institution of marriage. I had married David, and his appointment as the Commanding Officer of one of the Navy's helicopter squadrons led him to be on standby to deploy to Afghanistan in 2001. David's belief was that it was his duty to follow orders and deploy at a moment's notice, and my belief was that his duty was to our son (and me). Thoughts of divorce and single parenthood began when two SA80 rifle magazines crashed onto the kitchen floor along with the rest of his personal equipment waiting to be packed. Having gone through the process of questioning the military system during my own career, I was able to point out how its power, mightier than the individual, would devour whatever we were prepared to give. On this occasion it was our marriage that was at stake.

It was during this very personal conflict that we both experienced the force greater than that of military might. We uncovered it not in the fanciful realms of romantic love, but firmly rooted in the fundamental principles we discovered we shared regarding the future of our son. Since then both of us have recognized this force on occasions when we have understood our personal limitations and the boundaries they impose. When we uncover issues over which we have wildly differing views we are able to challenge one another openly and honestly. Having become rooted in the knowledge that we will eventually come to an amicable agreement, we know that the reconciliation of our differences continues to strengthen our relationship. An example of this came in the summer of 2002, when the issues raised by David's career came to the fore again. On 11 September, we attended the launch of Peace Direct (the conference and performance of *Transforming September 11th*) at the Royal Opera House. I was delighted and honoured to be with a Royal Naval Officer of 22 years who was willing to explore my new direction. As the music danced around the auditorium linking stories and people with emotions and truths, the hearts of those willing to experience raw compassion were flung wide open. I reconnected with the inner joy I had lost around the time of the first Gulf War and celebrated the new connections that were seemingly all around, by allowing myself to be on an emotional high. I felt ready and able to create a future that is different from my past.

Then on 21 September, we were at the Royal Naval Air Station, Yeovilton, on 'Air Day' where I watched David fly in his part of a simulated hostage rescue subsequent to a terrorist takeover. It felt as though my soul was being bombed. Sights, sounds and smells of the aircraft rumbling around in the sky, the simulated gunfight, and the voice of a mother shouting at the top of her voice, next to her four-year-old child, 'Shoot the baddies,' triggered a flashback to my time on active service to the point that I was no longer aware of my real surroundings. It wasn't the first time it had happened and the experience left me mentally and physically disorientated and frightened.

I contacted the Ex-Services Mental Welfare Association —
Combat Stress. Help from one of their welfare officers who
visited me on two occasions enabled me to unpack a part of my
mind, and process the emotions that had become stuck. I was
relieved to discover that despite everything my mental health is
sound — well, just as sound as any mother of a two-year-old!

I consider being a mother a greater challenge than anything I
was ever presented with during my time in the RAF and, furthermore, an opportunity for learning how to transform everyday
conflicts. I recall the days during the 2003 Gulf War; I felt alone
and began to doubt my belief that there are credible alternatives
to violence. I felt angry when I knew my very personal memories
of the war were causing feelings of discontent to accumulate in
my body. Ordinarily I'd find solace with a friend who for a few
moments could share my experiences, but I could find no such
friend around. I had been glued to the news of the war on the
television when my two-year-old child's eyes engaged with mine.
'Mummy, are you happy?' he asked. In a small voice I said, 'No
sweetheart, I'm not.' My hope flooded back as he instantly
replied, 'You watch this, you won't be happy!' Immediately my
attention returned to my role as his mother, shocked that I had
found myself wallowing in my anger, and fear of pain and death
triggered constantly by the media's interpretation of the war. My
anger subsided and the impact of his uninhibited wisdom enabled
a sense of calm to replace the tension in my body.

It was in a book on parenting that I read about violence being
anger gone wrong, and that anger applied positively can be a very
useful motivator. I began to see how this can be the case and

started to resume my research into peaceful alternatives for resolving conflict. I reread Professor Adam Curle's work in *War Prevention Works — 50 stories of people resolving conflict.*[2] I was reconnected with his words about our acceptance of the current culture of profit, power, fame and achievement seeping into the collective mind, and that it has defaced and turned away from our universal inheritance the qualities of wisdom, courage and the capacity for love.

I wrote to him. His reply, by return, built on the hope and love restored in me by my child, at a point of near despair when I was relying on the television for my knowledge. Although I know it's impossible, it grieves me that I am unable adequately to express my understanding of love amongst these words. I feel it to be a force of elemental proportions that has no respect for the frailty of the human mind, and that by embracing it unconditionally I can live life again, with a healthy respect that all I have could be taken away from me in an instant.

Now, I make conscious efforts to turn off the television and seek to inform my opinions from sources rich in new knowledge and understanding. I am currently researching the mediation process and how it can be applied to so many areas within everyday life. And I am convinced that if individuals are serious about conflict resolution, then it is a real place to start.

It is nearly five years since I left the Royal Air Force, and within months David will leave the Royal Navy. I am beginning to feel physically, mentally, emotionally and spiritually healthy again. I no longer feel powerless, no longer hindered by the words *'theirs not to reason why, theirs but to do and die'* ('Charge of the Light Brigade',

Alfred, Lord Tennyson). I cherish and enjoy my freedom to question and feel privileged to be part of a society that allows this freedom. I believe that civilians and the military have much to learn from one another, and it is my hope for the future of the twenty-first century that the pathways for young people's careers will include gates that are as inviting to pass through as those of the military were for us in the twentieth century. After all, when stripped of our material gain, we are simply men and women endeavouring to build solid foundations from which future generations can begin their journeys through life with peace and security.

Notes

1 Jones, E.G., 'Women in Combat — Historical Quirk or the Future Cutting Edge?', in Elworthy, S., *Power and Sex,* Rockport, MA: Element, 1996, p. 29.

2 Mathews, D., *War Prevention Works: 50 stories of people resolving conflict,* Oxford: Oxford Research Group, 2001.

Scilla Elworthy

Scilla Elworthy is the founder and chair of Oxford Research Group, established in 1982 to develop effective methods whereby people can bring about positive change on issues of global and local security by nonviolent means. She is also the acting executive director of **peace direct**. *Scilla has spent the past ten years bringing policy-makers together with independent experts to develop ways past the obstacles to disarmament, control of the arms trade and greater global security, and has been nominated three times for the Nobel Peace Prize. Previously*

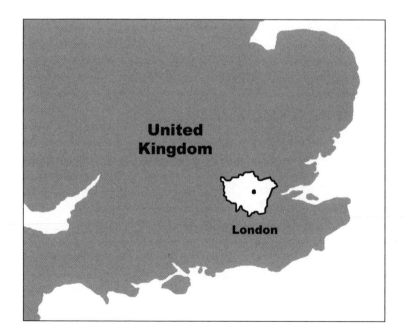

she was a consultant at UNESCO on women's issues, director of Minority Rights Group in France and worked for ten years in southern Africa. She is also the author of many publications; Power and Sex was described by Vogue magazine as '... essential reading for anyone concerned with the future of mankind'. In January 2003, Scilla met with ministers in Baghdad to discuss a possible way out of the crisis. In May of the same year, Scilla was awarded the Niwano Peace Prize.

I was born into a military family. My father served in the British Army in the First World War, my eldest brother was a para-trooper and another brother was in the Royal Navy. I was the youngest of five children brought up on a farm; it was a wonderful life, lived almost entirely out-of-doors in tune with the changing seasons.

Then the world fell apart. My beloved brother was killed in a car accident. He was ten years older than me and I respected him and trusted him absolutely. He disappeared so suddenly and so acutely, leaving me a heart cracked open by pain and aloneness.

As children we were taught to shoot and to kill birds, rabbits, hares and foxes. When I was 13 years old I was given a shotgun. I was rather competitive with my four big brothers. To prove how tough I was, I went out into the woods with the gun and did something absolutely forbidden. I pointed it upwards from below at the nest of a jay, and pulled the trigger. Eggs, nest and pieces of the mother bird showered down on me. One beautiful blue jay's feather landed in my hair. I was profoundly shocked by what I had done. I don't think I told anyone.

At around that time (1956) the Hungarian people rebelled against the Soviet Union. Soviet tanks thundered into Budapest to quell the revolt, and on our grainy black-and-white television I watched kids my age throwing themselves at the tanks. I was pinned to the spot by their courage. I went upstairs and packed my suitcase to go and join them, and my mother came and told me not to be silly.

The feeling of awe at the raw courage of people who refuse to be cowed by brutality or oppression never left me. When I was 16 I spent my summer holiday working in a rest home for survivors of Nazi concentration camps. One old man, who had the mark of a boot across his face, offered to teach me to draw and I sat listening to him for hours. Later I worked in camps in France for Vietnamese refugees, and in Algiers with children orphaned by the civil war. I felt shocked that life had offered me so much, and for others life was so relentlessly hard. I was stunned by how people who had lost everything — their parents, loved ones, their history, their possessions — still stayed alive, still survived, even smiled. I wanted to understand how the human spirit does this.

However, when I got to South Africa on my travels, the good life became irresistible. I got a job as advertising manager for a chain of dress shops, earned a fortune, bought a sports car, modelled for Mary Quant and took almost no notice of what was going on around me. It was only after I married and had a baby daughter when I was 30 that core life challenges visited again. I fell ill with a brain disease called encephalitis, which put me in a coma, apparently destroying a quarter of my brain cells, and left my head in a fog for six years.

All I wanted to know when I emerged from the fog was the answer to the questions 'Who am I?' 'What am I here for?' These have been the big issues for me ever since, so I'm grateful to that illness for changing my life. At that time, in the late 1970s, such questions were considered a bit daft and only very odd or sick people went to psychotherapists. So, not for the first or last time, I was considered very odd. I became passionate about self-knowledge, especially the approach taken by Carl Jung using myth, legend, dreams and symbols to help understand the psyche and enable the unconscious to become more conscious.

I began to work for the Minority Rights Group, and helped a group of African and Arab women carry out a research study of female genital mutilation. This was the first time such a painful subject had been brought to public notice, and I was then asked by UNESCO to undertake some research work for them. This time the subject was 'The Role of Women in Peace Research, Peace Initiatives and the Improvement of International Relations', about which I knew absolutely nothing. But I soon found a number of women from all parts of the world who knew a lot, and together we produced a series of seven case studies that became UNESCO's contribution to the second UN Conference of Women in Copenhagen in 1980. These case studies opened my eyes wide. Whether from N. Ireland, Cuba or the Philippines, the women in them had this extraordinary quality of fearlessness in the face of terror that so magnetizes me.

The British peace movement was at that time coming out in protest at the Reagan/Thatcher nuclear build-up, and women who had wheeled pushchairs all the way from Wales chained themselves to the gates of Greenham Common Airbase, where US Cruise missiles were to be stationed. I felt a sense of outrage that these provocative missiles were to be added to an arsenal that could already obliterate the planet and everyone on it. I felt fury that we were taking such risks with the fragile, mysterious, beautiful eco-system that we are a part of. I felt afraid too for my eight-year-old daughter and her generation.

Up to that time, I had listened and studied and pondered, but I hadn't really acted. This was partly because every time I thought of something to do a voice in my head said, 'You can't do that.' I didn't know then that this was the voice of fear, which tells lies. It was also partly because, like so many people, I didn't know what I could do that would have any effect.

Nevertheless, I joined the protests, marched, organized and, in 1982, was in New York lobbying on behalf of British NGOs (non-governmental organizations) while the UN was holding its Second Special Session on Disarmament. After an inconclusive week, a vast demonstration against nuclear weapons took place in the streets of New York filling Central Park with a million people. The *New York Times* gave it five pages. It was totally peaceful. 'This,' I thought, 'will change everything.' Back in the UN the next day, not one government had changed its position one inch. It was clear to me that people in offices making decisions on weapons were not listening to the people on the streets pouring out their anguish and fear. I was pondering all this while strap-hanging on a tram on Broadway, when suddenly I had an idea. What if we could find out who actually made decisions on nuclear weapons — who designed them, commissioned them, built them, paid for them, strategized with them, deployed them — and what if we put the people on the street in touch with the decision-makers person to person? Surely the power of their concerns, sincerely expressed in a real conversation, would be persuasive?

So I came home and set up a research group round my kitchen table. What became the Oxford Research Group started as me and two friends and a manual typewriter with a French keyboard; we knew so little about weapons that we started with a pack of cigarette cards illustrating various missiles. We persisted, enrolling specialists who did know how things worked in the various countries, drawing up organizational charts and cross-checking names in the CIA open files on the shelves of specialist libraries in London. For funds we managed on seed funding from Quaker charitable trusts. After four years MacMillan published our first book, entitled *How Nuclear Weapons Decisions are Made,*[1] which had chapters on each of the nuclear nations and included organizational diagrams for the relevant posts in the weapons labs, the ministries of defence, the military, the intelligence services, the defence contractors.

We began putting groups of concerned citizens — women's groups, church groups, groups of doctors and lawyers — in direct touch with the decision-makers we had identified. Not everyone was pleased. Stones came through windows with unpleasant notes attached, the apartment of our researcher in Paris was searched by men in raincoats, our phones were bugged, and when I took my car to the garage they pointed out that the tyres had been neatly slit all around the inside. We decided then that the only way to deal with secrecy was through complete transparency. Our commitment was to render accountable a process usually veiled in secrecy. We believed that if the public knew what was being decided behind closed doors, they would not endorse it. The only country that did hold a public debate over whether to develop nuclear weapons was Sweden, and the public answer was an emphatic 'no'.

In 1988 we published a *Who's Who*, offering 650 biographies of the key nuclear weapons policy makers in the US, the Soviet Union, Britain, France and China. At that point doors closed on us. The top civil servant in the UK Ministry of Defence (MoD) sent out an instruction that no one in the Ministry or the Armed Forces was to speak to or have anything to do with anyone connected with Oxford Research Group. Our then publisher Frances Pinter was served with a 'D notice' forbidding publication of the book, but she went ahead. Newspapers stopped publishing articles about us, and invitations to appear on radio and television almost dried up.

All this time, inside myself, I was struggling with conflicting feelings. These were feelings of self-doubt and inadequacy, that I had no business to be meddling in all this, alongside a passionate conviction that nuclear weaponry was too dangerous to be developed and deployed as we were doing. So, this official 'dismissal' only served to reinforce the voice inside my head that had been saying for years, 'You're an upstart. How dare you challenge experienced, respected people who know what they're doing? Why can't you behave, and do something normal?' I began to realize that that was an internalized voice from childhood, probably my father's, who was distant and inaccessible to children, and very critical. I saw that what I was up to was partly an attempt to heal that early lack of recognition, by trying to communicate with and influence powerful men.

This realization was painful, because it felt childish, but it did help me to be clearer and more honest in what I was doing. At that point, we started carrying out a series of in-depth interviews to try to discover the assumptions behind the need to build more nuclear weapons. I wrote to ministers and former ministers of defence, generals, air marshals, CEOs of weapons manufacturers, scientists and civil servants, asking if they would agree to consider questions such as 'How do you perceive the threat?' on condition of anonymity. Some of them never replied; 13 agreed. These interviews often went on for several hours and were fascinating. We listened as they talked about enemy capability versus enemy intention (this was when the Soviet Union was breaking up), about deterrence, about what provided people with security.

After the Berlin Wall came down, I went back to the same people and interviewed them again; almost none had changed any of their views. I wrote up the study for my doctorate at the University of Bradford. The unplanned and unexpected result of this research was that by the early 1990s a dozen or so senior defence figures now trusted us. We began to invite them to speak at meetings, and to join in round table discussions on specific aspects of policy, like how Britain could respond to the substantial US and Russian agreements to destroy quantities of (largely obsolete) nuclear warheads. We always invited a number of well-informed critics of nuclear policy, like scientists who had previously worked at Aldermaston, so the discussions were very lively and very focused. For every policy-maker who agreed to come to one of our meetings, there were at least three who refused, and every refusal felt to me like a failure. It took me a long time not to take it personally.

It was always difficult to feel that we were making any progress, especially because, after all the hopefulness at the end of the cold war, by 1998 India and Pakistan had both developed nuclear weapons, and some of the established nuclear nations began to design smaller, 'usable' weapons. Also there was no way of measuring whether the conversations we were having were making any difference; people don't usually tell you if something you have said may have caused them to rethink. But there were some signs.

In 1995 we were invited by the Chinese to take a delegation to Beijing as part of an on-going series of exchanges that I had initiated a decade earlier, when I had first had a hunch about how important a role the Chinese were going to play. On each visit the seniority of the delegates was ratcheted up, and on this occasion I invited General Sir David Ramsbotham, former Adjutant General of the British Army and an extremely independent man who would have no truck with the MoD's instructions about us. He agreed to come, and so did a rear admiral, an air vice marshal and the head of West German military intelligence. We also took with us several independent critics of both Chinese and British nuclear policies, including the head of Greenpeace nuclear campaigns division who had been arrested in Tiananmen Square three weeks previously. We were given a banquet in the Great Hall of the

People, and at the end of the week's discussions, as an enormous honour, we were invited to meet the top generals of the Chinese armed forces. I did feel as though we were getting somewhere. The Foreign Office told us later that for several years the Oxford Research Group had been the only bilateral channel of communication between the UK and China on nuclear issues. The critical voices inside my head were notably quiet, for a week or so.

You do have to know your stuff to engage in the world of defence decisions, and as a woman you have to know it better than average. In a way, I suppose, it helped to be competitive and to want to 'keep up with the boys'. As time went on I began to be less fearful of getting it wrong, of not knowing my facts, of not being able to answer a question put to me at a military institute. The fear lessened, I believe, not because I was more knowledgeable but because I was less fearful generally. That in turn was because I was beginning to learn how to go 'through' fears in my personal life. Once, after having been woken in the early hours night after night by the terror of losing someone I loved, I finally sat up in bed and shouted at the terror, told it to come here and sit down and explain itself. It never bothered me again.

I realized that fear tells lies. Fear does that. It concocts scenarios in your head of terrible things that might happen, and they are nonsense. They prove to be false. But if you believe them and give them energy, they often come true. So I found that I had to try to be quicker off the mark than fear, to notice when it was spinning a story in my head and, once I had noticed, I could just laugh and it stopped. As I understood myself better and became less afraid, I became more interested in the policy makers *as people,* rather than as the incumbents of posts.

When you think about nuclear weapons, the problem can seem so huge it's easy to be daunted and feel one can do nothing. What we tried to do was break it into bite-sized pieces, then invite people to get to know a lot about a small part of it — the part for which one person held decision-making responsibility. We would then develop a dialogue with that person, as a fellow human being. We tried to bring a sense of humanity, of the personal, into this most political of issues — it is after all about life and death.

In May 2003 I was invited to Tokyo to be given the Niwano Peace Prize, and as I sat in the auditorium as the ceremony began I became aware of my father's presence at my side, although he has been dead since I was 18. He seemed to be crying, something I had never witnessed in life, and I realized he was weeping with pride. Something changed for me in that moment. I felt a kind of inner healing, as though he recognized me for who I am. In that instant I knew, at least in part, the answer to the question 'what am I here for?'

Note

1 Elworthy, S. (ed.), *How Nuclear Weapons Decisions are Made,* London: McLain, 1996.

You have been telling people this is the Eleventh Hour.

Now you must go back and tell the people that this is the Hour.

And there are things to be considered:Where are you living?

What are you doing?What are your relationships?

Are you in relation?Where is your water?

It is time to speak your Truth. Create your community.

Be good to each other, and do not look outside yourself for a leader.

This is a good time!

There is a river flowing now very fast. It is so great and swift that there are those who will be afraid.They will try to hold on to the shore.They will feel they are being torn apart, and they will suffer greatly. Know that the river has its destination.The Elders say we must let go of the shore, push into the middle of the river, keep our eyes open and our heads above the water. See who is there with you and celebrate.

At this time in history, we are to take nothing personally, least of all ourselves: for the moment we do, our spiritual growth and journey come to a halt.

The time for the lone wolf is over. Gather yourselves! Banish the word 'struggle' from your attitude and vocabulary. All that we must do now must be done in a sacred manner and in celebration.We are the ones we've been waiting for.

Message from the Elders of the Hopi nations, Oraibi, Arizona, 2 December 2001.

YOU CAN DO THIS TOO

Living in a difficult world

by Dina Glouberman

When I read these stories, I become aware how protected I have been in my life from some of the horrific experiences described in these pages. Of course I have suffered in many ways and on many levels, but I haven't lost a family member to a bomb, or gone blind in an explosion, or watched my people shot at and abused. Do I have a right to consider myself in the same category as these courageous people?

Yet there are also people speaking in these pages who have not had such violent experiences. They too feel deeply touched by the way the world is and isn't, and have devoted their lives to being of service in ways that can inspire us all. Neither the pain nor the joy of living and of giving has to begin with any particular life situation in order to be real and of value.

How can we see the process of becoming of service as one that applies to us all? These are some of my thoughts, and some questions I have asked myself — and am inviting you the reader to consider too.

World pain touches all of us

We all participate in world pain, the pain of being human in a difficult world, in some form or other, whether through our own personal and family experiences or through our relationship with the experiences of others with whom we have empathy. No one is exempt. No matter how comfortable our personal lives may be, we cannot help but be touched by the violence, pain, illness, unhappiness, inequality and misunderstanding that makes the world a difficult place. Deep in our soul we have always known that there is pain and conflict around, whether it is talked of or not, and that this pain and conflict has an impact on us, whether or not it seems to involve us directly.

Some questions to think about:

• *How does the pain of the world touch you?*

• *How do you insulate youself from the pain of the world?*

•*What kind of pain have you suffered that has forced you to think about what you can or must do to stop the pain, either in you or in others, or in the world?*

•*What is the first picture that comes to mind?*

We all try to defend ourselves from that pain

When we come face to face with severe pain, whether personal, family, cultural, political or spiritual, our first response is often to close down, close in, get stuck, attack ourselves, become hopeless, blame others and even seek revenge against those we feel are responsible. We are pushing for a quick closure that we hope will stop the terrible pain. Yet if we do so, we get stuck in a cycle of pain and retribution that cannot easily end.

Some questions to think about:

Think of a time when someone or some group or institution said or did something that hurt you.

• *What picture comes to mind?*

• *How did you try to stop that pain?*

• *What was your first reaction?*

• *Your second? Your third?*

It's hard to avoid looking for instant answers

Despite urgency of a situation, while we need to stay engaged we also need to wait:

1. Hold off from an early resolution, and surrender to all our feelings.
2. Hold off from blaming ourselves and others and surrender to a not knowing.
3. Hold off from hopelessness and keep the faith that we will be OK again.
4. Hold off from defending our old stories and tell ourselves the truth.
5. Hold off from our narrow identifications and surrender to a recognition that we are part of a larger whole.

The little mantra I find useful, which evolved out of my work with people who are burning out, is to say: *Wait. Give up hope. Keep the faith.* This means that we have to stop holding it all together, give up the hope that things will ever again be the way we thought they were or expected they would be, and yet keep the faith that whatever happens we will ultimately be all right.

Waiting does not mean that we can't act until we understand everything. Sometimes we need to act on what we do already know and be prepared to keep learning.

Another little saying I have is: *The truth hurts but it doesn't harm. It is illusions that kill.* All of us lie to ourselves when we are attached to some way of seeing ourselves or the world that we don't want to give up at any price. Yet unless we let go of our investments in how things used to be and put truth first, whatever our truth may be, we cannot truly emerge into the larger picture.

Think of a situation in the past or present that you believed or believe must be dealt with right now or else something terrible could happen. Picture yourself in the middle of it.

•*What is at stake externally?*

•*What could happen to you personally if it does not work out?*

•*What happens if instead of acting and reacting you stop, breathe, tolerate the anxiety or the pain, suspend judgement, refuse to have a quick answer, let yourself know the whole truth and just wait until some resolution comes from deep inside you?*

Try it.

We can't do it alone

It takes courage to let go of deeply held beliefs and emotions and open to a bigger picture. It takes courage to risk losing the approval of those individuals and groups who have been important to us. In order to hold us during this time when we may feel frighteningly cut off from our moorings, we need a *soul com- munity*. This means that we must reach out to people who accept us for who we are and who we are becoming, rather than what we have been or should be, or achieve, or represent. This also means that we need to find people who care about what we care about, in order to work on things together. These people will be concerned with those basic human values that lead us to feel part of the world.

Our soul community can support us to find the strength to tell ourselves the truth, face our inner and outer challenges and do what we need to do. Some of them will even dream with us, plan with us and act with us.

Many of us are used to taking charge and making things happen, and have the view that if we don't do it ourselves, it won't get done. Yet, the time of superman or superwoman is over. We can't do it alone. But we are not alone. We are part of a living, developing whole.

Here comes the joy

It's hard to believe it at the moment when things are painful, confusing, stressful or frightening, but amazingly, when we really face

Some questions to think about:

• *Who is there in your life right now with whom you feel fully yourself no matter how you are feeling, what you may be doubting or believing, and what you are doing or not doing?*

• *Which people who are now absent or dead, or which spiritual teachers, or authors, or literary or historical characters, or which animals or symbolic beings, could inspire you, love you and guide you during difficult times?*

• *What about people around the world whom you may not know personally but are part of the same loving struggle?*

Imagine that you are surrounded by a protective, loving circle of these people or beings. Do your thinking and feeling and planning in this protective circle.

Now join the circle and talk to them in your mind. Where possible, seek them out in reality and begin to share on a level you haven't dared to do before. Gain love and guidance. Offer love and guidance. Join forces to dream or plan or act. Don't be apart. Be a part.

the truth, and reach out to others in that truth, something remarkable happens.

Somehow we discover that what we are feeling is not personal but the collective pain of the human condition, and that it is not the whole picture. As we dare accept that things are as they are, and that we are as we are, and that the process is working itself out in its own best way, we may find strange flowers blossoming in the cracks of our consciousness. And as we begin to feel that we can be part of the process in our own best way, and that we are in alignment with our deepest self, doing what we are meant to do, the flowers burst out with a vibrancy and colour that can take our breath away.

These flowers are the blooming of our joy, the love of life itself. While pain is collective, joy is universal. It blossoms in the spaces of our life even when all else fails. It is the biggest picture of all.

Wading our way through difficult emotions and relationships

by Francesca Cerletti

In reading these stories I am deeply moved by the depth of the emotions portrayed — emotions that I can recognize from my own experience of personal and work conflict. The more we can relate these stories to our own experiences, the more we can easily find out what we can learn from them. For example, less than two years ago, I found myself, rather abruptly and unexpectedly, in the middle of a conflict that tore my family apart. I had put an enormous amount of energy into trying to help my father who was in serious financial trouble, and now my integrity and honesty were being questioned by one of my brothers. None of my training or my professional work in conflict management had quite prepared me for this. I became convinced that it is not so much the emotions themselves but the way we deal with them that will influence the outcome.

There is a tendency to view interpersonal conflict as negative. In truth, it can be an extremely positive source of creativity and energy. Much rests on our ability to listen to our feelings, acknowledge them and channel their energy into something positive. When I was in the middle of the situation, it seemed the end of the world; I was cornered with no solution, no future. Amongst a turbulence of emotions, I felt scared, angry and totally powerless. When I had cried enough, and despaired enough, I suddenly remembered what I had learned in my studies and in my work, and began to look for ways to turn what was happening into something that could be called positive. Like the people in this book, I embarked on a voyage of personal discovery, of understanding, and rapprochement with others which is still going on.

As it is hard to find creative solutions in moments of stress and heightened emotions, it is useful for us to consider in advance how we can look at painful situations and turn the turbulence into something that can open up dialogue and new possibilities. To do so, we need to observe not only our own emotions but also our relation to the other with whom we are in conflict.

'Although attempting to bring about world peace through the internal transformation of individuals is difficult, it is the only way. Wherever I go, I express this and I am encouraged that people from many different walks of life receive it well. Peace must first be developed within an individual. And I believe that love, compassion, and altruism are the fundamental basis for peace.'

The Dalai Lama

Where am I in this situation?

Some questions to reflect upon. Allow any images or pictures to emerge when you ask yourself these questions.

•*What is conflict for you?*

• *How has it arisen in your own life?*

• *Are you aware of any particular triggers that make you very reactive maybe deriving from how difficult situations were dealt with in your childhood?*

• *How do you actually feel in situations of conflict?*

• *How do you deal with your emotions?*

Anger

When chaos broke loose in my own life, after the initial shock I felt really angry and bitter. What was I to do with these flashes of violent emotion? Was I to let rage guide my hand and hit my brother? Or was I to use the rush of energy for something useful?

Anger can take many forms. What is most important is the direction that it motivates us in. For example, anger may sometimes take the form of a complaint: 'It's not fair. How could they do this to me/them?' This leaves us feeling bitter and powerless. Anger can also close us up deep inside, or it can lead to hatred that escalates the situation and can even lead to violence. This violence can become self-perpetuating.

However, anger can also work as a fuel which provides us with energy and motivation to act positively. Eventually it can be transformed into the passion we need to commit ourselves to whatever path we choose to take.

For example, anger and pain at first almost destroyed Bud Welch. This anger soon turned into a desire for vengeance — wanting the bomber dead without a trial. Then, however, his feelings changed. He looked at his anger and realized that vengeance would not bring his daughter back to life and even the death of the bomber would resolve nothing. From then on, his commitment was to work against the death penalty. This path also brought him a sense of healing. It was far more rewarding to work for reconciliation than for revenge.

Similarly, Terry Kay Rockefeller looked at her anger and realized that she needed to distinguish the anger itself from the desire for revenge. She saw that the implications of going down the route of vengeance would mean further death and destruction. Instead, she too chose the path of reconciliation.

> **'An eye for an eye leaves everyone blind.'**
> Martin Luther King

The key is to pause when angers kicks in, listen to all our feelings, understand why we are angry, and honour the feelings without moving directly into action or reaction. Feelings are different than judgements or decisions. As we understand and validate our feelings, we can also make a choice about how we will channel them instead of being driven by the heat of the emotions.

Fear

Jo Berry in her account talks about fear: fear of the outcome of the first meeting with Pat Magee, fear of having chosen a path which could have been interpreted as betrayal, fear of having made the wrong decision, fear of being unable to sustain the implications of the path undertaken.

Fear of what is unknown or risky is a natural response 'programmed' into us by nature to protect us by giving us a 'default' option to fight or to flee. This was particularly useful at the origins of our species when dangers from predators were a constant threat to our survival, as the adrenalin rush created by our system enabled us to run faster or put up a good fight. Understanding our fear, therefore, enables us to work with it. This does not mean that we will not feel the fear, but that we will be able to channel the extra energy into productive/constructive actions.

There is also the fear of failure or of taking the wrong decision. Yet failing and getting things wrong from time to time is part of our nature. If we let this paralyse us, we go nowhere. We need to acknowledge our mistakes and learn from them, but it is equally if not more important to treasure those experiences that have had positive results. Understanding and valuing what enabled those successful outcomes will allow us to use what has worked well at the moment we most need it.

The decision to work nonviolently often goes against our own conventional thinking and often that of the social group we identify with. It may even break serious taboos. This can be enormously threatening to our identity as the person who we have been. It is not surprising that we are frightened.

'Whatever you do, you need courage. Whatever course you decide upon, there is always someone to tell you that you are wrong. There are always difficulties arising that tempt you to believe your critics are right.'

Ralph Waldo Emerson

So, do we need to be heroes? What kind of courage do we need?

Interestingly, the consciousness of being a 'courageous' person ('I am courageous, therefore I can do') was not at the forefront of the thinking of the people who tell their stories here. They did not consider themselves especially brave while they were doing what they did; they did what felt right for them. If you asked them, they would all say they were ordinary, frightened people who listened to their emotions and took one step at a time. Jo Berry, amidst anger and pain, was frightened of what her encounters and the route she was pursuing could bring, but she went on.

It is here that the courage lies, in the ability to face our feelings, acknowledge the pain that may come to us or those around us, and yet make the decisions we feel are right and follow them through. Even one step can be crucial. We will not feel like heroes, and yet it is a heroic choice.

Sometimes we need to remember that we are not alone in our fear. Carmel McConnell told me of her experience of the protest at Greenham Common. She had met with other women and they discussed their concerns. One by one, each admitted they were seriously frightened of being arrested and going to prison. As they shared their fears, it became a common bond, and they carried on in spite of it — even because of it.

Sometimes we have no choice but to act in courageous ways that we might have thought were not possible for us. There is a famous anecdote about Aung San Suu Khi, the Burmese leader who, unarmed, walked straight up to the machine guns of the soldiers who had been ordered to shoot the demonstrators she was leading. Their safety catches were off. Their fingers were trembling on their triggers. But still she walked, until she was able to gently put her hand on the barrel of one soldier's gun. The tension suddenly defused.

Aung San Suu Khi must have been frightened. Who wouldn't be? But she refused to let this overpower her. If she had, a great many people would have been killed.

> **'The law of love will work, just as the law of gravitation will work, whether we accept it or not.'**
> M. K. Gandhi

Power

The feeling of not being able to influence the course of events in the direction we believe is right can be a source of frustration, anger, even humiliation. Rachael Burgess tells of how demeaned and powerless she felt in the face of the overwhelming power of the military system she was part of. So many of us feel that we have no power over policies or procedures, or the way strategies are set in our workplace or governing bodies, and we can despair at our powerlessness.

We are not all-powerful, and there are many things we have no control over. That does not mean we are powerless, however.

What is important is to focus on what we can directly influence. As we do this, we begin to sense that personal power that we have which no one can take from us.

In my own case, while I was sitting with my family, watching events unfold, I felt totally in the grip of someone else's manoeuvring. I was paralysed, angry and full of hatred. However, when I managed to channel my anger and act in the way I felt was right, I lost my feeling of powerlessness even though I didn't immediately change anything in the situation.

Even when we cannot immediately change what is happening in our environment, we can change something about ourselves — the way we think, behave, communicate and act. Rachael Burgess resigned. In so doing, she started a journey from feeling powerless to a new sense of freedom. The crucial shift was in her recognition that her power resided in the ability to change her own life.

> **'Human beings, by changing the inner attitudes of their minds, can change the outer aspects of their lives.'**
> William James

Remarkably, as we change, people around us do indeed start changing, first in the way they relate to us and then in the way they act themselves. The situation cannot possibly remain the same when we are different. This can be a start.

Once we recognize our sphere of influence and work within it, we can also extend its reach. Scilla Elworthy from her round-the-kitchen-table beginnings has now become a reputable source in the eyes of the Ministry of Defence and the Government. Most success stories start very simply.

'The power of a waterfall is nothing but a lot of drips working together.'
Michael Maynard and Andrew Leigh

Who is the other?

Some questions to reflect upon — there is a sequel to this exercise later on, it might be useful to make some notes:

• *How do you feel about the other person or group in a difficult situation?*

• *Do you ensure that he/she/they feel heard? How?*

• *Do you try to see how the other might be feeling? How?*

• *Can you listen to and value the other's perspective while holding on to what is true about your own position?*

Try this:

Imagine changing seats and sitting in the place of the 'other'.

• *How do you see yourself from this new position?*

Now return to your own seat.

• *What have you learned?*

In situations of conflict or tension often we build barriers that exacerbate the situation. Often this is because we fear that if we let down our barriers we will be exposing ourselves to danger or saying we are wrong. Yet this simply increases the danger. How can we break stalemates and negative spirals?

> 'There lies before us, if we choose, continual progress in happiness, knowledge, and wisdom. Shall we, instead, choose death, because we cannot forget our quarrels? I appeal as human being to human beings: remember your humanity and forget the rest.'
>
> Russell-Einstein Manifesto

Comprehension

Understanding something or someone does not automatically mean justification, acceptance or agreement with that particular issue or person. You are simply acknowledging and honouring the fact that they too have sincere reasons for believing and acting as they do.

This is very clear in Jo Berry's and Pat Magee's stories. They understood each other's path, but Jo does not condone the bombing and Pat does not disown his action. Yet their ability to understand each other's position created a bridge between them, opened a door to dialogue and friendship, and eventually had an enormous impact on both their lives and on their work. Whatever Pat Magee says about the past, he is now committed to a nonviolent approach.

In fact, as in Pat Magee's story, people often turn to violence because they feel that they are not being heard and will never be heard. The less we are listened to and understood, the more rigid we become. Once we feel heard, we may even feel ready to relax and find a new way forward.

> **'Peace cannot be achieved through violence, it can only be attained through understanding.'**
> Ralph Waldo Emerson

'Humanizing' the 'other'

Realizing that the 'other' is a human being, who has feelings, a family, hopes, expectations helps the reconciliation process. This recognition is evident in almost all the stories and was an integral part of the internal journey to look for alternative solutions to violence.

Dave Grossman,[1] a US military officer, historian and psychiatrist, explains how in training soldiers, dehumanizing the enemy is an integral part of making people into efficient killing machines. The 'other' is turned into an abstract entity. The opponent is transmuted in a faceless 'they', constructed by officialdom and narratives of the system.

Anat Levy Reisman tells us that in order to see and understand 'the other', she needed to revisit and deconstruct the narratives created by years of antagonism.

This does not only occur at the collective or institutional level. It may also happen in the workplace. How often do we say, *'They* haven't done this,' etc. The question for us, then, is: 'Who are "they"?'

Humanizing the other will also help us to move away from an abstract view of the situation and bring it down to a more human dimension in which we have the power to interact. We not only honour the other, but we feel less powerless ourselves.

What do we have in common?

Once we are able to see 'the other', and understand that he or she is often motivated by values (justice, freedom, inclusion etc.) and needs (security, livelihood), we begin to see that we have some things in common. I remember a song by Sting at the time of the cold war, 'Russians'. It went: 'Russians love their children too.' When I first heard it I clicked that people often act because they care. This doesn't mean that I have to justify those actions. The fact that we have values in common, despite their different implications, may enable us to work towards mutually acceptable solutions.

A relevant example for us could again be the workplace when we can get heated up with one of our colleagues about the way to do something. We both are committed to what we are doing and want to do it well (this is why we get angry). What we disagree on is, often, the interpretation of processes and procedures. Discovering what we have in common gives us a basis to start communicating.

Seeing the future

Often people in conflict have difficulties in visualizing a post-conflict future. In conflict we may get stuck in the present — there is only now. The ability to project oneself or the conflicting parties into the future in concrete terms helps to break up the stalemate of anger, revenge and the past. A question often asked in mediation is, 'What will the future look like when you have settled your dispute?' From the stories, for example Amjad Jaouni's and Pat Magee's, it is possible to see that a particular turning-point for them was the thought of their children and the need to secure them a future.

There is always a future. And we will need to live it, one way or another. This realization may encourage us to think about how we would like to live it.

It's not personal

This follows from the last exercise, in which you were asked to look at the other's viewpoint and at your own position from the perspective of the other.

It is now time to let go of both positions.

Step out into the position of an observer looking at both.

• *What is happening?*

• *What do they have in common?*

• *Where do they differ? How?*

• *What would you advise each of them?*

As observers of any interactions we may be in a position to understand the process of how those interactions unfold. Similarly, in situations of conflict, if we were able to distance ourselves from what is happening we would be able to gain a new perspective that enables us to transcend the situation. What we would probably notice is that often in conflict we are players in a drama that began before us, or that it is not about ourselves as human beings. Being able to distinguish the nature of the conflict from a personal attack helps us to give up any vested interest in who we believe we are. Then we can act effectively.

Finding our own way

It is clear from all the stories that it is necessary to honour and acknowledge our feelings and emotions, not simply to act. But there is no single way to deal with our emotions and feelings. Each of us has to choose our own path on our own terms. And so much depends on what the situation is, how much time we have to work our feelings through, and what is at stake at any moment. If we really do need to act before we have the time to fully consider the situation, let us at least hold onto an honesty that will enable us to evaluate our actions, recognize when we haven't been wise, and find a better way forward.

Notes

1 Grossman, D., *On Killing: the Psychological Cost of Learning to Kill in War and Society,* Boston: Little Brown, 1996.

You can do this too

by Francesca Cerletti

> 'One great thought can change the dreams of the world,
> One great action taken all the way to the sea can change
> the history of the world.'
> Ben Okri

Having read the stories, having considered what goes on in our inner life when we are confronted with a difficult world and how we might deal with the emotions and relationship issues that emerge, we may be asking: 'Now what? How can we begin to act? How can we find what to focus on?'

Sometimes the uncertainty of not knowing where to start, who to contact or whether we have the skills, the time and the strength can make taking action seem daunting. In putting together this book, we hoped to encourage and enable you, the reader, to start taking a first step towards making a difference in areas you are passionate and concerned about. What can we do to address those initial doubts and go forward?

Here are four basic steps that will help clarify your motivations, identify some of your key skills, think about assets available, evaluate your options and consider who else to involve. You may wish to read the section in its entirety and do the exercises suggested, or go directly to the parts that are of most interest to you.

Let's start.

Step 1: Motivations

What leads people to do something? What makes us, for example, decide to march against war or to work in the community to improve racial relations?

What drives each individual is different. Some of our 'unarmed heroes' started by embarking on an internal journey, looking for healing, understanding themselves, living according to their own values and expectations. For others it was the search of a better future or the wish to give what was received. Circumstances also played a part (meeting people, being in the right place at the right time or in the wrong place at the wrong time). For example, Ben Mussanzi wa Mussango's faith in God and love for his people inspired his belief that there were alternatives to violence and led him to set up the *Centre Résolution Conflits* and train people in conflict management.

Whoever and wherever you are, you can do it.

What the protagonists of our stories have in common is that they were normal human beings. Although some have been affected by exceptional circumstances, others have not. In this they show that experiencing a personal tragedy is not a prerequisite to taking action. The strongest motivation comes from what one believes in.

Individuals in the past acted on their conviction, for example the early campaigners against slavery, and the suffragettes. This is their legacy to me. What will be mine to my grandchildren's generation?

The first step is to clarify what we most value and believe in: something that we feel the world around us should reflect.

Thinking about what we value and believe in relation to who we are, our life-styles and choices, will help us to articulate what we are passionate about. Thinking about what needs to happen in the world around us for those values to be true will enable us to identify what we can personally contribute and prioritize where we should channel our energy.

This becomes our driving force.

> **'Be the change you want to see in the world.'**
> M. K. Gandhi

Where do I start?

Asking the following questions will give you a clear start. Give simple answers and don't spend too long on them. Some will find jotting notes useful.

• *Who are you?*

• *What do you value most?*

• *Do you live according to these values (and why)?*

• *Are you prepared to make the necessary choices to sustain what you believe in?*

• *Does the world/environment around you reflect what is important to you?*

• *What do you want to happen?*

• *What can you do to start making a difference?*

This is your starting-point: write it here in CAPITALS!

Remember — no one in the stories started with a big bang. Everyone started by doing very small things, mainly questioning himself or herself. For most of those who told their story the path to action began while searching for answers and questioning whether they lived according to their values. It was the encounter with 'the other' that prompted Anat Levy Reisman's reflection on her values and whether she lived according to those values. For Rob Green it was the tension arising between his commitment to the Royal Navy and the knowledge that Trident outstripped UK requirements which underpinned his resignation. Bud Welch and Martin Snoddon each embarked on a journey to reconcile the moral dilemmas they were experiencing. 'Small' is a beautiful way to start.

If you would like to make your passion an integral part of your career you might want to read: McConnell, C., *Soultrader. Find purpose and you'll find success,* London: Pearson Education, 2002.

Step 2: Skills

Once you have identified your motivations and objective, the next step is to look at your skills.
You do have the resources!

Each and every one of us has particular skills that we regularly use. We listen to our friends, organize events, analyse situations, write reports, administrate family finances, etc. Often, however, we just do things without paying attention to how we do it. It is in the detail of how we carry out tasks, achieve goals and deal with situations that our skills reside. What we need to understand is how we use them in relation to different situations, so that we can draw on them to achieve what we have set out to do.

How do I do it?

You may want to do this exercise with another person as if it were an interview.

Think of a time when you felt you achieved something in your life (or think of a time when you did something that made you proud and gave you a feeling of fulfilment). This could have happened in any sphere of your life: at home, at work, with friends, with the family or even alone. It could be making something, writing a speech, organizing a dinner, talking to your children, helping your neighbour, achieving a goal, understanding something.

Try and visualize the moment. What was the day like, what were the sounds, the smells, were there cars, were you alone etc.

Close your eyes and go back to that moment. Then, trying to be as detailed as possible, answer the following questions.

Describe the event/experience.

• *What was it about you that enabled you to reach this achievement: the way you worked, the ideas you had, the way you behaved?*

• *What were the skills, the experience, the knowledge, the resources you drew on?*

• *What made this an important/significant event?*

• *What was it about the environment, the situation that enabled you to be successful?*

• *Were other people involved? If so what was their role? How did they contribute?*

• *What did you value most about the others?*

• *What did you value most about yourself?*

This is your starting-point. This experience gives you clues about *your* skills, resources and knowledge, which you can draw on to take action.

Step 3: Becoming an Activist

Your starting-point is determined by:

- Your vision.
- What you believe you can do to make a difference.
- Your skills.

How do you actually start?

There is not just one single way to become an activist — it varies. Ben Mussanzi wa Mussango chose to set up the centre as a way to help people learn how to live together and deal with the conflicts that affect their lives. Scilla Elworthy decided to work within the system to challenge it. Her strategy has been to influence institutions and policy makers using the avenues and tools established by them rather than frontally attack them.

Be passionate, be bold.

You have to choose what works best for you. Everyone in this book followed what felt right for him or her. What enabled each person to get where they are also differs. They have all taken different routes. Some, like Douglas Sidalo, have been encouraged by others and have capitalized on their support. Maria Mangte 'exploited' her position as a former People's Liberation Army member and prisoner of the Indian military to become a conduit to build bridges between the two.

Identifying the assets, resources and connections you have is a way to begin. This will also help you to evaluate your options.

Assets and options

Use these questions as prompts for reflection:

- **What are your assets and resources? You may find it useful to write a list.**
  Physical assets
  Financial assets
  Time

Consider also those which may be less apparent, for example where you live or if you own a car. Your geographical location may facilitate access to other resources or information, while owning a car might enable you to deliver and distribute things. Also remember to consider emotional assets like the ability to care — showing that you care will win people over.

- **What are your options?**

You will then need to consider the implications of each. These can range from the resource requirements, your time availability, how other people will be affected, and the impacts in the short term and in the long run, etc. You may want to make notes or use the table provided.

Remember to include: 'do nothing'. This is also an option, which, when you will evaluate its implications, will provide further clarity on your intentions/motivation. Also think of the advice they give on planes: the nearest emergency exit might be behind you. Therefore consider easy or obvious things, like joining other groups, which might prove to be the most effective way for the time being.

Option	Advantages						Disadvantages			
	Resources necessary	Time required	Impacts	Potential Outcome			Resources necessary	Time required	Impacts	Potential Outcome

The relevance others may play in your life as an activist can be extremely important. Kathy Kelly and her experiences were instrumental in Colleen Kelly's commitment to nonviolent action as the only worthwhile response to September 11th.

People may also help practically. Sometimes what is more important is not what you know, but to know someone who does know what you don't. Starting from this premise, think about your network of people and how they can help you.

Whom can I involve?

Reflect on the following questions. Opposite is an 'action helper' format you may wish to use.

• *Who do you know?*

• *Do they have the same feelings and care about the same things as you do?*

• *What do they know?*

• *Do they have skills which complement yours?*

• *Do they have access to resources (not only money, it could be faxes, email, photocopying, space to meet)?*

Remember — Share, be inclusive and build trust. This may be one of the greatest assets you have.

Name	Cares about	Knowledge	Skills	Resources	What could they do

You may also want to consider getting in touch with existing groups and organizations and asking their help and advice. To provide you with a starting-point, in the Resources section of this book we have indicated links and listed some of the organizations involved in some way in conflict resolution.

Take the first step and the rest will follow.

Step 4: Learn from what you do

Whatever happens, remember to treasure the experience.

'You learn from your mistakes'. True. But you especially learn from what goes well. Not many of us remember this fact. So, don't just flog yourself when something goes wrong, making a point not to go there again. Celebrate your successes and identify what has made them possible and use it in moments of difficulty.

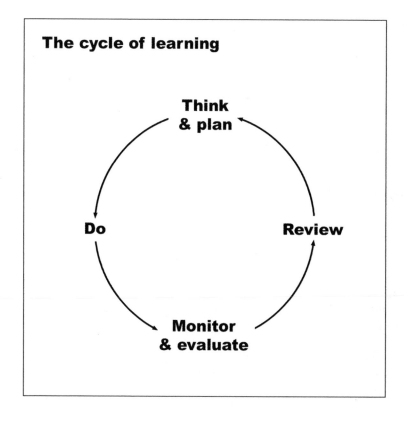

The cycle of learning

Think & plan

Do

Review

Monitor & evaluate

What have I learned?

One way is to use a similar format to the 'How do I do it?' exercise.
Below is another suggestion. Otherwise use what you feel it is most
appropriate.

• *What happened?*

• *How did it happen (the sequence of events, the skills, resources, and the
knowledge used)?*

• *What went well?*

• *What was different?*

• *What surprised me?*

• *Who was involved? How did they contribute?*

• *What did I learn?*

• *How can I use this in the future?*

Health Warning

Be persistent

Expect to meander and be patient: the road is winding. You are
dealing with people, behaviours, cultures, attitudes, etc. Change
takes a long time and often you will have to endure setbacks, but

this does not mean everything is lost or has been futile. Try, try, and try again. There is a point at which actions that seemed previously to have absolutely no effect suddenly take root.

Further reading: Oxford Research Group, *Everyone's Guide to Achieving Change. A Step-by-Step Approach to Dialogue with Decision Makers*, Oxford, 2002.

Store up energy

You will need loads of stamina. Evaluate carefully how much time you can give. Follow Martin Snoddon's example: take care of yourself, remember your family and friends — go out for a meal!

Joy over sorrow

In the book there has been much talk about anger, pain, bitterness and vengeance. These realities are very real. More importantly, however, those who have engaged in this new path have found that their efforts have been compensated by a sense of fulfilment and joy. Choosing this path is not only about healing. The knowledge of being able to make a difference, however small, is also rewarding.

Next steps and concluding thoughts

We hope that this book has been inspiring and has provided useful tips for you to take your interest further. If you have identified your mission, the best advice we can give you is: *Get out and do it! The only way to do it is to **do it**.*

This is how we, at **peace direct**, started. With an idea in mind of helping those who chose nonviolent ways to resolve conflict, we looked for people who could support it and put it into practice. Then we took the plunge and began work.

peace direct has linked people and groups to work together for peace. For example, we have linked conflict resolution workers in the most violent areas of the Democratic Republic of the Congo with an individual in London who has helped to raise funds towards a conflict resolution centre in the country as well as training in nonviolence. We have connected up a web designer in Wales with a network of conflict resolution practitioners in Africa to enable them to build and develop their website, thereby facilitating the sharing of their experience and skills.

Today **peace direct** is raising money to enable the headmaster and two students from the City Montessori School in Lucknow, India, to come to the UK. Members of the school played a prominent role in calming inter-faith violence that erupted in their city after the Ayodhya mosque was destroyed in 1992. We would like them to open a dialogue with the communities of cities like Bradford and Oldham, sharing their experiences of living where communal tensions can be high.

peace direct is also arranging media interviews for a British Iraqi who is setting up a citizens' centre in Kirkuk (north of Baghdad) to provide support and assistance to those who have lost relatives, been raped or suffered illegal arrest subsequent to the war.

These are just a few examples of what we are doing. (Please see our website for the latest.) If you are interested in what we do or have comments and thoughts about this book, or would like to become involved with **peace direct**, we would very much like to hear form you. It could be the simple way to take your first step. Do contact us (see details on p. ii).

'I like to believe that people in the long run are going to do more to promote peace than our governments. Indeed, I think that people want peace so much that one of these days governments had better get out of the way and let them have it.'

Dwight D. Eisenhower

The prevention and resolution of conflict using nonviolent methods

by Scilla Elworthy

The stories in this book demonstrate how people, as well as communities or nations, get caught up in deadly cycles of violence. These cycles are deadly because they ensure that one conflict leads straight into another, often involving more and more killing.

The classic cycle of violence has roughly seven stages. This cycle has been evident in the Israeli-Palestinian conflict, in central Africa and repeatedly in different regions of former Yugoslavia.

The diagram opposite shows how the cycle of violence works in the human psyche, and it is at a human level that conflict prevention should operate, because the origins of the cycle can only be dismantled within the individual human mind and heart.

Breaking the cycle

Intervention is needed at the point before anger hardens into bitterness, revenge and retaliation. To be effective it must address the physical, the political and the psychological security of people trapped in violence; all are equally important, and one without the other is insufficiently strong to break the cycle. In every case,

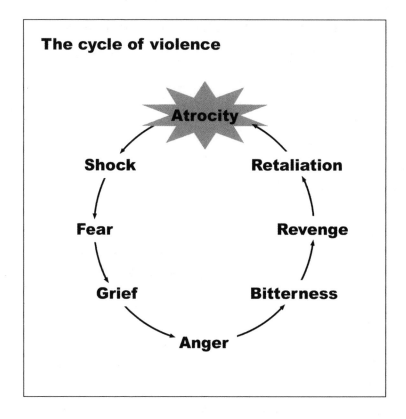

the people involved in situations of violence must be supported in the development of their own resources for transformation. We will now illustrate what is meant by interventions for physical, political and psychological security, giving four examples in each case. (This essay is concerned with conflict resolution or mitigation initiatives *per se,* and does not attempt to include reference to the profoundly important role of relief, development and human rights agencies.)

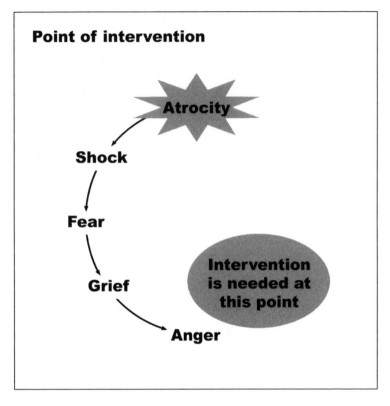

Intervention for physical security

Peace keeping

Where people have murdered, brutalized or tortured each other, the first necessity is to keep them physically separated. Strategies for peacekeeping are developing through the harsh experience of the tragedies of Rwanda, Bosnia, Kosovo, East Timor, Somalia, Cambodia and Cyprus. The consequences of late intervention, inadequate intervention or no intervention at all (as in the case of Tibet, Burma, Iraq, the Israeli/Palestinian conflict, Sri Lanka or Kashmir) are becoming clear. There is now an extensive body of knowledge and training on this subject, developed by the United Nations, independent research institutes and many national armed forces.[1]

Many peacekeeping operations have been hindered by problems preventing them from achieving the desired results. These problems include the operational mandates (Bosnia), timely availability of sufficient resources and competent personnel, and permission from the relevant heads of state to operate in-country (East Timor). However, as stated innumerable times by Kofi Annan, Secretary-General of the United Nations, the principal obstacle to effective UN peacekeeping is the level of political will among the members of the UN Security Council, especially the permanent five (P5). But, where peacekeeping operations have sufficient support, they prevent bloodshed and perform the essential task of creating an environment in which peace building and reconciliation can take place.

> … if we are given the means — in Kosovo and Sierra Leone, in East Timor and Angola — we have a real opportunity to break the cycle of violence once and for all.[2]

Protection
When civilians are threatened, driven from their homes, or under attack from militias, they can effectively be protected in a number of ways. One is by the introduction of trained civilian violence monitors, as in the case of Kosovo by the Organization for Security and Cooperation in Europe (OSCE), a regional intergovernmental organization with 55 member nations. For the six months prior to the NATO decision to bomb Serbia, the OSCE

had deployed 1300 monitors throughout Kosovo. The monitors were from all over Europe, their job to check and report on instances of intimidation or ethnic violence.

> The mission, staffed by more than 30 nations, is being loaded with ... tasks: maintenance of the ceasefire, separation of the military forces, mediation of disputes, protection of human rights, collection of war crimes evidence, building up of democratic institutions and holding municipal elections.[3]

There is good evidence to show that everywhere the orange Land-Rovers of the OSCE went, violence stopped. It was precisely at the point when these monitors were withdrawn and the bombing began that the wave of killing and eviction began in earnest.

Another form of protection is provided by NGO initiatives like the Peace Brigades International (PBI), who mobilize and provide trained units of volunteers in areas of high tension to help discourage violent outbreaks. This kind of intervention only works when the aggressor knows that enough of the international community supports the protectors. For example, in Colombia in 1995, where there had been 38,000 political assassinations over a four-year period, PBI sent teams to provide round-the-clock unarmed protection for prominent human rights activists whose colleagues had been killed, abducted or tortured. One such activist said:

> The death sentence against each and every one of us has not been carried out only because we have had Peace Brigades International accompaniment.[4]

This work has shrunk the 'impunity space' — the space available for repressive regimes for violent and illegal action. American citizens undertook similar work in Nicaragua in the 1980s with an organization that became known as Witness for Peace. In addition to living in villages at risk of violence from the Contras, Witness delegations, enjoying the relative protection that their nationality offered them, soon began following the Contras with notepads and cameras to record everything they saw. In some places their work took the form of taking testimonies from those who had been brutalized by the Contras. The same organization provided video cameras for use by nonviolent autonomous activists in north-east India to prevent abduction and murder by security forces. Peter Gabriel, co-founder of Witness, says:

> A camera in the right hands at the right time at the right place can be more powerful than tanks and guns. Let the truth do the fighting.[5]

Arms export controls

Embargoes or sanctions against the supply of arms to areas of conflict rarely work, for a number of reasons. These could effectively be addressed if:

- Supplier countries agree and police a binding code not to supply to areas where conflict is imminent, and impose penalties for supposed end users who resell arms.
- Substantial funds are provided, possibly through a tax on corporate suppliers, to introduce effective boundary controls on gun-running, and severe and enforceable penalties.

- The permanent five members of the Security Council cut their arms exports. Over the last five years, the United States has sold $50bn worth of major conventional arms, Russia has sold $16bn, China $1.5bn, the United Kingdom $7bn, and France $11bn.[6]

As in the case of nuclear weapons, the P5's refusal to exercise restraint has led to other countries following their example. Germany and the Netherlands now have energetic arms exports, encouraging the excuse, when a large sale is pending, 'if we don't supply them, someone else will'. That argument was used to justify slave trading. An international treaty to control and reduce arms sales is essential if terrorism, by state or non-state parties, is to be dealt with. NGOs such as Saferworld and Oxfam have helped secure a European Code of Conduct limiting arms exports.

The second rationale put forward for justifying arms exports is the necessity to protect jobs in the defence industry. This argument, repeated so often that it has assumed the status of a national myth, has comprehensively been shown to be false. In a report published in July 2001, and unchallenged since, research showed that each job in UK defence exports costs the British taxpayer £4,600 per annum, and that instead of contributing to the economy, or even to the effectiveness of HM forces, arms exports are a net drain on the British economy, and the favouring of British suppliers has led to inferior equipment.[7] The same subsidies, applied to new products in the fast-growing environmental sector, would be more productive and would better support the wider British economy.

Gun collection

When a country is awash with weapons after a civil war, effective schemes are needed to collect and destroy the weapons. This has been undertaken in recent years by the United Nations in Albania, by NATO in Macedonia, and by individual initiatives in other countries. For example, in El Salvador in 1995 a group of businessmen whose trucks were being hijacked by heavily armed gangs (as a result of twelve years of civil war) copied a successful initiative from the Dominican Republic. For every gun surrendered they offered food vouchers worth $100. By the end of the second weekend vouchers worth $103,000 had been issued, despite the organization having only $19,500 in available funds. In view of the success of the programme, the president of El Salvador intervened to help, and in three years over 10,000 weapons were handed in.

Intervention for political security

Law enforcement is a prerequisite of stabilization, whether before, during or after major conflict. It is now widely recognized that strategies for security sector reform must take an integrated approach. The UK Government's approach to the security problems in Sierra Leone show that an integrated strategy can be very effective. In this case, four government departments, the Department for International Development (DfID), the Ministry of Defence (MoD), the Home Office and the Foreign and Commonwealth Office (FCO) addressed different aspects of security sector reform:

- DfID funded activities in support of civilian control of the security sector;
- MoD helped to develop a national security policy, including the reorganization of Sierra Leone's defence ministry, and training the army;
- the Home Office provided personnel skilled in managing reform of police services; and
- the FCO helped to fund military education and training.[8]

Unless the legal and coercive instruments which a citizen encounters are perceived as legitimate and independent, then the capacity of the state to implement policies intended to support reconciliation and prosecute human rights violations will be severely undermined. For example, during South Africa's transition to fully democratic post-apartheid politics, a lack of faith in the criminal justice system was a significant obstacle to progressing towards the new political regime.

> ... it was widely perceived that apartheid crimes could not be handed over to the old criminal justice system. The whole edifice of a culture of human rights and equal citizenship rests upon the existence of a 'state of right', which involves an end to the arbitrariness and irrationality of a repressive juridical apparatus and the establishment of due process and fairness.[9]

Free elections

The removal of a dictator and installation of the democratic process is a monumental task. This was certainly so in the case of Slobodan Milosevic, named by the International Crisis Group as the 'single greatest cause of instability and conflict in southeastern Europe'. In July 1999 the US-based East-West Institute and the Slovak Ministry of Foreign Affairs brought together the representatives of pro-democracy forces from the Federal Republic of Yugoslavia, including trade unions, NGOs and independent media. A task force was set up to assist all those working for change who had been active, even against terrible odds, during the war. They built a coalition eventually known as the Democratic Opposition of Serbia, which was able to build a common strategy united behind one candidate, Vojislav Kostunica. With extensive election monitoring and a wave of nonviolent protest when Milosevic attempted to annul election results, the Democratic Opposition of Serbia won the Serbian elections.

The extent to which a population values the opportunity a free election provides to express the popular will, especially when the population has previously been denied democratic rights to political participation, can be clearly demonstrated. For example, in 1999 the UN Assistance Mission in East Timor (UNAMET) undertook voter education and registration for the referendum in which the East Timorese would decide between independence from Indonesia or a form of autonomy. Despite the increase in violence by militias against the civilian population prior to the election, an astonishing 98 per cent of the electorate voted.

> Enthusiasm, even joy, was widespread, as it always seems to be when people are given the first chance to vote in their lives.[10]

The fact that the election results were preceded by an increase in violence illustrated in a terrible way just how significant the free election was. Such an incontrovertible public assertion of the will of the people could not be ignored by those so bitterly opposed to this process.

Control of militias

Armed militias or paramilitaries have to be brought to the negotiating table. This is not necessarily best done by armed forces; in many instances NGOs or respected civilians have succeeded. For example, in Mozambique the Community of Saint Egidio, supported by the Vatican, became involved in a series of meetings with leaders of FRELIMO and RENAMO, culminating in October 1992 in the signing of a comprehensive peace accord. This provided for the demobilization and reintegration of combatants, the creation of a new Mozambican Defence Force, and the creation of political parties and freedom of the press. The United Nations was given the responsibility of overseeing the transition from war to peace which led to the first free elections in October 1994.

Free press

An independent media is essential to the prevention of war. Conversely, hate radio can inflame conflict to white heat, as happened in the Rwandan genocide. In nearby Burundi in 1994, violence began to spiral; the main radio station was controlled by the state, whose army had been complicit in the violence. With the aid of the US-based NGO, Search for Common Ground, the independent 'Studio Ijambo' was launched early in 1995. In spite of one of the team members being killed by the army, they continued their balanced news coverage, proposing solutions to the crisis facing the country. In two years they produced 2500 features on peaceful co-existence and a soap opera to which after four years 85 per cent of the entire population was listening. Studio Ijambo has received many international awards for its role in calming explosive tensions, defusing rumours, and promoting reconciliation.

During the operation of the United Nations Transitional Authority in Cambodia (UNTAC), it soon became clear that the only way UNTAC was going to be able to communicate their message in the face of systematic intimidation by the Khmer Rouge and others, particularly to communities in the rural areas, was by radio.

> The broadcasts of Radio UNTAC helped offset the political impact of the violence of the regime and the threats of the Khmer Rouge. It became one of the most successful components of the UN's operation in Cambodia. For the first time Cambodians had a free and unbiased source of information, and nearly the entire population became avid listeners.[11]

Intervention for psychological security

Witness

The traumas experienced by victims of atrocity need attention and, if possible, healing. One way in which this is done simply and effectively is by a technique called 'active listening', whereby an independent witness or witnesses gives the traumatized person their full attention for as long as necessary to discharge their fear, grief and anger. This simple technique takes time and care, but done well it prevents anger hardening into bitterness and retaliation. In Croatia, for example, in the midst of the war, a group of citizens set up the 'Centre for Peace, Nonviolence and Human Rights' in Osijek. Today it has grown into one of the largest citizen-led peace-building organizations in the country. The centre sends 'peace teams' to towns and villages to aid the healing of trauma which has left so many people emotionally scarred. In places where Serbs still live, the peace teams have made important progress in reducing the level of animosity and tension between Serbs and Croats, thus reducing the probability of violence breaking out anew.

In every conflict, there are those willing to risk their lives to build a nonviolent solution. Such people are often community or church leaders, and frequently women. There are a multitude of examples, including: the initiative of Liberian women to bring about disarmament before elections from 1993 to 1997; the Women's Organization of Somalia who emerged in the midst of war to prepare the groundwork for peace; the Mothers of the Plaza de Mayo, mothers of the disappeared in Argentina who helped transform a fractured and violent society; and the Women of Wajir in north-eastern Kenya. Their motto was:

> You must commit yourself to continuing the peace work no matter what happens: if my clan were to kill your relatives, would you still work with me for peace? If you can't say yes, don't join our group.

Their intervention was the key to ending an inter-clan war by setting up public meetings and rapid response teams. It was so successful and cost effective that it has now been copied in other parts of the country, coordinated by a special representative in the office of the Kenyan president.

Bridge building

The efficacy of bridge-building between communities fractured by decades of violence has been most evident recently in N. Ireland, where it has long been recognized that support for community bridge-building is an essential element of efforts designed to overcome deeply ingrained community hatred and suspicion, with particular attention being paid to schoolchildren. For example, during the late 1980s and early 1990s Education for Mutual Understanding, an educational working group, was established which sought to enable children to: learn to respect and value themselves and others; appreciate the interdependence of people within society; know about and understand what is shared as well as what is different about their cultural traditions; and appreciate the benefits of resolving conflict by nonviolent means.[12] They aim, through education and inter-school programmes, to assist children's understanding of their cultural heritage and common experience. The project originally operated only in one district of N. Ireland; the organizers worked out that to extend the project across the province, it would cost £1.39m, or 0.25 per cent of the annual education budget.

In India there are many potent examples of bridge building. In the slums of Ahmedabad, a small NGO called St Xavier's Social Service Society has worked for years in fostering a climate of inter-religious understanding between the desperately poor

Muslim and Hindu communities. By targeting false rumours before they spread, by setting up 'peace committees' made up of local people and by proactively addressing the root causes of the tensions between Hindus and Muslims in the slums, St Xavier has undoubtedly made a significant contribution to inter-religious coexistence in the area.

The lies, suspicion and betrayals which characterize war can fester for decades and erupt in further atrocity if not addressed. This needs to be done in public and in a safe and controlled environment, and one of the most effective is a Truth and Reconciliation Commission. To date there have been 20 of these, each building on the lessons of the last, the most well known being held in South Africa from 1995 to 1998.[13] The process, when properly conducted, goes far deeper than any superficial bargaining for amnesty. The South African constitution of 1993 talks of the importance of reconciliation and reconstruction:

> [they provide a] secure foundation for the people of South Africa to transcend the divisions and strife of the past, which generated gross violations of human rights, the transgression of humanitarian principles in violent conflicts and a legacy of hatred, fear, guilt and revenge.[14]

The demands of reconciliation with a view to ensuring a peaceful transition to a democratic society often necessitate postponing or rationing justice for the victims and families of gross human rights violations. In place of conventional justice involving legally sanctioned punishment for crimes committed, efforts are made to expose the egregious acts and systematic violations of the past and to establish accurate and detailed records of them. Debate over the efficacy of Truth and

Reconciliation Commissions often revolve around the requirements of expediency and the imperatives of justice and law. Nevertheless, truth and reconciliation commissions do perform a vital reconstitutional function within transitional democracies, and help to break the cycle of violence. It is extremely painful for all concerned, but when the truth is really told it can help to bring about a transformation so substantial that deep reconciliation is far more likely to be achieved.

In concluding this section on intervention for psychological security, we would emphasize that it is the most frequently neglected, perhaps because it is considered 'soft', yet the power of change in the human heart is formidable. It is what can transform violent activists into statesmen. The development undergone by Nelson Mandela during his years on Robben Island, after he was convicted of terrorism, made it possible for him to emerge from jail unshakably committed to negotiation and reconciliation. Had it not been for the depth of his and his colleagues' conviction, there were enough people on both sides ready to fight for South Africa to have been plunged into a civil war which could have cost millions of lives. The same is true of Alistair Little, who joined a Protestant paramilitary organization in N. Ireland aged 17, shot a man point blank and spent the next twelve years in the Maze prison; it was there that he witnessed the fatal hunger strike of Bobby Sands. It moved him to the core that a Catholic could care so passionately about his cause as he did, and kill himself in the process. The depth of this experience was such that since his release 13 years ago Alistair has worked full time and often unpaid for reconciliation and bridge building between Catholic and Protestant communities in N. Ireland.

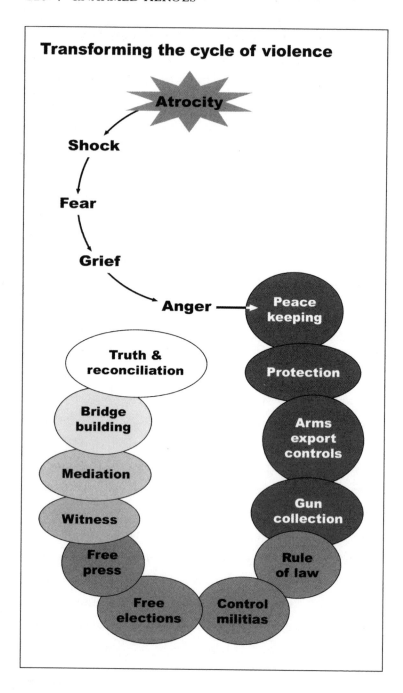

Transforming the cycle of violence

These brief examples, taken from thousands of interventions around the globe, indicate the potency of nonviolence. If applied systematically, robustly and with adequate funding, these methods illustrate how the cycle of violence can be transformed.

There are two final points to be made about breaking the cycle of violence. The first concerns evaluation. There are now at least 51 institutes and other centres in the United Kingdom researching conflict resolution, from Sandhurst to Bradford University, and knowledge of what works and what does not is growing fast.[15] While increasingly efficient measures of evaluating conflict resolution initiatives are being developed, the fact remains that if they are successful, it is hard to measure what did not happen. Conflict prevention at its most effective will enable those involved to avoid bloodshed, possibly even a full-scale civil war, with all the associated destruction. A method of calculating or assessing the value of prevention, or of comparing the relative effectiveness of military and civilian intervention, has yet to emerge. This is a challenge for governments, intergovernmental agencies and NGOs alike.[16]

The second point is that interventions such as these described above, while increasingly the subject of research, are inadequately funded. The UK Government has undertaken some laudable initiatives, including the funding of conflict prevention measures through the collaborative efforts of three ministerial departments. Yet we still allocate to non-military interventions less than 2 per cent of the funding allocated to the military.

What, in essence, is nonviolence?

Right at the end of this book, let us be quite clear what nonviolence means. Whereas we all now know about 'endangered
species' or hunger or recycling, there is no similar familiar strategy
for people to know what they can actually DO about peace. Peace
tends still to be a bit vague, seen as desirable but idealistic.

So obviously it is necessary to examine nonviolence, what it is
and what it is not. In combat you are risking your life to kill
others; in nonviolence you are risking your life (if necessary) so
that others will not be killed. This requires rigorous training and
deep conviction; the effect it has on violent, cruel or angry
people is more powerful than more violence. It affects them at a
profound level. It is the force of Satyagraha, developed by Gandhi
and entirely successful in driving the British out of India. The
practitioner renounces the use of force, voluntarily and on
principle, and replaces it with determination combined with
compassion, combined with courage. Gandhi himself said:

> What Satyagraha does is not to suppress reason but to free it from
> inertia and to establish its sovereignty over prejudice, hatred, and
> other baser passions. In other words it does not enslave, it compels
> reason to be free.

This is the power Martin Luther King taught and used to vast
effect in desegregating the deep South. It is what Aung San Suu
Khi used when she walked unarmed straight up to the machine
guns of Burmese soldiers who had been ordered to shoot the
demonstrators she led. It is what Nelson Mandela developed dur-

ing 27 years in jail and used to prevent a civil war in South Africa on his release. It was the power behind the 'Velvet Revolution', which brought down the Iron Curtain. It was the power that deposed General Pinochet in Chile, Slobodan Milosevic in Serbia and, more recently, Schevardnadze in Georgia.

Professor Michael Nagler, founder of the University of California Peace and Conflict Studies programme, estimates that nearly one third of the world's people have practised some form of nonviolence, or 'life force', for the redress of grievances,

> This is the concept of 'people power'. The idea is that the power of an aroused populace is greater than the power of the state, since the state depends on the consent and the cooperation of its citizens. And when citizens rise up, as they notoriously did in the Philippines twice in recent memory, the state is powerless to stop them. But people power is only the tip of the iceberg. The real nonviolence, in my understanding, is person power. That is, the power of the single individual.

And that is what this book is all about.

Notes

1   Titles on peacekeeping include: Shawcross, W., Deliver Us from Evil: Peacekeepers, Warlords and a World of Endless Conflict, London: Bloomsbury, 2001; Rose, M., Fighting for Peace, Time Warner, 1999; Gordon, S., and Toase, F., (eds.) Aspects of Peacekeeping, London: Frank Cass, 2001; United Nations General Assembly Security Council, Report on the Panel on the United Nations Peace Operations, A/55/305, August 2000.

2 Annan, K., quoted in Shawcross, W., Deliver Us from Evil: Peacekeepers, Warlords and a World of Endless Conflict, London: Bloomsbury, 2001, p. 376.

3 International Herald Tribune, 27.1.99.

4 Mathews, D., War Prevention Works: 50 Stories of People Resolving Conflict, Oxford: Oxford Research Group, 2001, p. 55 (many of the examples which follow are taken from this volume).

5 Ibid. p. 97.

6 Stockholm International Peace Research Institute, SIPRI Yearbook 2001, Oxford: Oxford University Press, 2001.

7 Ingram, P., and Davies, I., The Subsidy Trap: British Government Financial Support for Arms Exports and the Defence Industry, Oxford and London: Oxford Research Group and Saferworld, 2001.

8 Understanding and Supporting Security Sector Reform, DfID Guidance Report 2002.

9 Wilson, R.A., in de Britto, A.B., et al. (eds), The Politics of Memory: Transitional Justice in Democratising Societies, Oxford: Oxford University Press, 2001, p. 201.

10 Shawcross, W., Deliver Us from Evil: Peacekeepers, Warlords and a World of Endless Conflict, London: Bloomsbury, 2001, p. 355.

11 Ibid., p. 76.

12 See http://cain.ulst.ac.uk/issues/educ/init.htm (cited 28 August 2002).

13 See following link for discussion of truth commissions: http://www.iss.co.za/pubs/mongraphs/no68/chap11.html# anchor-4158 (cited 28 August 2002).

14 Hesse, C., and Post, R., (eds), Human Rights in Political Transitions: Gettysburg to Bosnia, Zone Books, 1999.

15 See Miall, H., Ramsbotham, O., and Woodhouse, T., Contemporary Conflict Resolution, London: Polity Press, 1999; Francis, D., People, Peace and Power: Conflict Transformation into Action, London: Pluto Press, 2002; Fisher, S., Ludin, J., Williams, S., Adbi, D.I., Smith, R., and Williams, S., Working with Conflict. Skills and Strategies for Action, London: Zed Books, 2000.

16 For a careful analysis, see Vayryen, R., 'Preventing Deadly Conflicts: Failures in Iraq and Yugoslavia', in Global Society, vol. 14, no. 1, 2000.

Further reading

Lederach, J. P., *Building Peace: Sustainable Reconciliation in Divided Societies,* Washington DC: United States Institute of Peace, 1997

Miall, H., Ramsbotham, O., and Woodhouse. T., *Contemporary Conflict Resolution,* Cambridge: Polity Press, 1999

Wallensteen, P., *Understanding Conflict Resolution: War, Peace and the Global System,* London: Sage, 2002

ACTION for Conflict Transformation, *Transforming Conflict, Reflections of Practitioners Worldwide,* Melville, South Africa: ACTION for Conflict Transformation, 2003

Fisher, S., Ludin, J., Williams. S., Adbi, D.I., Smith R., and Williams, S., *Working with Conflict. Skills and Strategies for Action,* London: Zed Books, 2000

RESOURCES

This directory of organizations and groups working in peace, conflict resolution and transformation has been grouped as **UK** *and* **Worldwide**. *Under the latter there are a vast number, and it is not possible to include more than a sample. At the end are links to web pages providing further links to organizations and resources.*

Organizations and Contacts in the UK

Amnesty International (AI)

A worldwide movement of people who campaign for internationally recognized human rights. AI's vision is of a world in which every person enjoys all of the human rights enshrined in the Universal Declaration of Human Rights and other international human rights standards.

> Amnesty International, 99–119 Rosebery Avenue, London EC1R 4RE
> Tel: +44 (0) 20 7814 6200 Fax: +44 (0) 20 7833 1510
> Website: www.amnesty.org

The British Council

The British Council's core objectives are to bring people and ideas together, and to work to contribute to peace education, training, exchanges and curriculum development in mediation and conflict resolution; to promote a responsible and critical media and through a cross-sectoral approach using creative arts as a vehicle for confidence building and communication between communities experiencing violent conflict.

The British Council have offices all over the world.
www.Britcoun.org.uk

For general enquiries:
Tel: +44 (0) 161 957 7755 Fax: +44 (0) 161 957 7762
Minicom: +44 (0) 161 957 7183
Email: general.enquiries@britishcouncil.org

For educational enquiries:
Tel: +44 (0) 131 524 5770
Email: education.enquiries@britishcouncil.org

Belfast
The British Council, Norwich Union House, 7 Fountain Street,
Belfast BT1 5EG Tel: +44 (0) 28 9023 3440 Fax: +44 (0) 28 9024 0341

Cardiff
28 Park Place, Cardiff CF1 3QE
Tel: +44 (0) 29 20 397 346 Fax: +44 (0) 29 20 237 494

Edinburgh
The British Council, The Tun, 4 Jackson's Entry, Holyrood Road,
Edinburgh EH8 8JP
Tel: +44 (0) 131 524 5700 Fax: +44 (0) 131 524 5701

London
The British Council, 10 Spring Gardens, London SW1A 2BN
Tel: +44 (0) 20 7930 8466 Fax: +44 (0) 20 7389 6347

Manchester
Bridgewater House, 58 Whitworth Street, Manchester M1 6BB
Tel: +44 (0) 161 957 7000 Fax: +44 (0) 161 957 7111
Minicom: +44 (0) 161 957 7188

Campaign Against the Arms Trade (CAAT)
CAAT is working for the reduction and ultimate abolition of the international
arms trade, together with progressive demilitarization within arms-producing
countries. It supports the promotion of peace, justice and democratic values,
and the use of the United Nations and civil society to resolve international disputes by peaceful means. CAAT also encourages policies to reorientate the UK
economy away from military industry towards civil production.

Campaign Against the Arms Trade, 11 Goodwin Street, London N4 3HQ
Tel: +44 (0) 20 7281 0297 Fax: +44 (0) 20 7281 4369
Email: enquiries@caat.demon.co.uk Website: www.caat.org.uk

Causeway

Causeway is an independent, non-party political, non-sectarian project devoted to conflict resolution through an exploration of the causes and effects of offence arising from the British/Irish conflict. It is inspired by and seeks to formalize the ongoing efforts of a number of former combatants and victims who, in discrete instances, have sought to reach out to the other and are aware of the transformative, healing effects of contact and cooperation.

Causeway, c/o Intercomm, 290 Antrim Road, Belfast BT15 5AA
Email: causeway29@eircom.net

Conciliation Resources

CR's organizational objective is to provide practical and sustained assistance to people and groups in areas of armed conflict or potential violence who work at community or national level in order to prevent violence or transform conflict into opportunities for social, economic and political development based on more just relationships.

Conciliation Resources, 173 Upper Street, London N1 1RG
Tel: +44 (0) 20 7359 7728 Fax: +44 (0) 20 7359 4081
Email: conres@c-r.org Website: www.c-r.org

Conflict Trauma Resource Centre (CTRC)

CRTC's mission is to contribute to alleviating the pain, suffering and trauma experienced as a result of the violent conflict in and about N. Ireland by way of cooperation and partnership across and between many boundaries to improve the quality of people's lives.

Conflict Trauma Resource Centre, Unit 9, Clanmill Arts and Small Business Centre, Morthern Whig House, 3–10 Bridge Street, Belfast BT1 1LU
Tel: +28 90 926060 Fax: +28 90 296050
Email: marc_n_Ireland@yahoo.co.uk

Dolphinton Dialogue Centre

A very exciting project is unfolding in Scotland close to Edinburgh Airport. On a 30-acre site, a centre of excellence will emerge that will offer a creative space for groups to engage in facilitated dialogue, develop best practice and learn the skills of dialogue for extending it to others. Currently funding is being sought for developing the buildings on the site but skilled facilitators of dialogue are available now to work with groups or organizations.

Tricia Boyle, Tel: +44 (0) 131 319 2224 or +44 (0) 131 319 2203
Email: patricia.m.boyle@btinternet.com

Edinburgh Peace and Justice Resource Centre

Resource centre for individuals and organizations interested in peace, justice and the environment.

Edinburgh Peace and Justice Resource Centre, St John's Church,
Princes Street, Edinburgh EH2 4BJ
Tel: +44 (0) 131 229 0993 Email: peace-justice@btconnect.com

FEWER, Forum on Early Warning and Early Response

The Forum on Early Warning and Early Response is a global coalition of organizations that provides early warning and promotes early, coordinated responses to violent conflict.

The FEWER Secretariat, Old Truman Brewery, 91–95 Brick Lane,
London E1 6QN United Kingdom
Tel: +44 (0) 20 7247 7022 Fax: +44 (0) 20 7247 5290
Email: secretariat@fewer.org Website: www.fewer.org

INCORE

INCORE was founded in 1993 in a joint initiative between the University of Ulster and the United Nations University. INCORE aims to address the management and resolution of conflict via a combination of research, training, and other activities which inform and influence national and international organizations working in the field of conflict.

INCORE, Aberfoyle House, Northland Road, Londonderry, BT48 7JA
Tel: +44 (0) 28 7137 5500 Fax: +44 (0) 28 7137 5510
Email:incore@incore.ulst.ac.uk Website: www.incore.ulst.ac.uk

International Institute for Strategic Studies

The IISS is the primary source of accurate, objective information on international strategic issues for politicians and diplomats, foreign affairs analysts, international business, economists, the military, defence commentators, journalists, academics and the informed public. The IISS's work is grounded in an appreciation of the various political, economic and social problems that cause instability, as well as the factors that can lead to international cooperation. It is an independent institute and it alone decides what activities to conduct. It owes no allegiance to any government, or to any political or other organization.

International Institute for Strategic Studies, Arundel House, 13–15 Arundel Street, Temple Place, London WC2R 3DX
Tel: +44 (0) 20 7379 7676 Fax: +44 (0) 20 7836 3108
Email: iiss@iiss.org Website: www.iiss.org

International Alert (IA)

An independent, international non-governmental organization that works at local, national, regional and global levels to generate conditions and processes conducive to the cessation of war and the generation of sustainable peace. They currently work with partner organizations and individuals in West Africa, the Great Lakes region of Africa, the Caucasus region of the former Soviet Union, Colombia, Sri Lanka, Nepal and the Philippines. They also conduct advocacy and policy analysis in the fields of business, development, gender, security and religion in relation to peace building.

International Alert, 346 Clapham Road, London SW9 9AP
Tel: +44 (0) 20 7627 6800 Fax: +44 (0) 20 7627 6900
Email: general@international-alert.org
Website: www.international-alert.org

The International Crisis Group

ICG is a private, multinational organization, with over 80 staff members on five continents, working through field-based analysis and high-level advocacy to prevent and contain conflict.

The International Crisis Group, London Office, Queen's Wharf,
Queen Caroline Street, London W6 9RJ
Tel: +44 20 8600 2538 Fax: +44 20 8600 2539
Email: kcronin@crisisweb.org Website: www.intl-crisis-group.org

Justice and Peace, Scotland

Justice and Peace (Scotland), 65 Bath Street, Glasgow G2 2BX
Tel: +44 (0) 141 333 0238 Fax: +44 (0) 141 333 0238
Email: justice_peace@virgin.net Website: www.justiceandpeace.org.uk

Mediation Northern Ireland

Originally founded as the Northern Ireland Conflict Mediation Association, the Mediation Network evolved in the 1990s as an agency to promote the practice of mediation and to train mediators in N. Ireland. In recognition of advances in the peace process and the growing diversity of mediation practice, the Mediation Network reorganized itself as Mediation N. Ireland in the autumn of 2002. They aim to be an independent centre of excellence in mediation and other methods of conflict intervention.

Mediation Northern Ireland, 10 Upper Crescent, Belfast BT7 1NT
Tel: +44 (0) 28 90 438614 Fax: +44 (0) 28 90 314430
Email: info@mediationnorthernireland.org
Website: www.mediationnorthernireland.org

Mediation UK

Mediation UK is working to promote constructive ways of resolving conflict within communities. They seek to ensure that everyone has access to high quality mediation and that the principles and practice of mediation are supported by decision-makers and the public, making mediation the first choice of method for resolving conflicts.

Mediation UK, Alexander House, Telephone Avenue, Bristol BS1 4BS
Tel: +44 (0) 117 904 6661 Fax: +44 (0) 117 904 3331
Email: enquiry@mediationuk.org.uk Website: www.mediationuk.org.uk

Minority Rights Group International

This is a non-governmental organization working to secure the rights of ethnic, religious and linguistic minorities and indigenous peoples worldwide, and to promote cooperation and understanding between communities. Their activities are focused on international advocacy, training, publishing and outreach.

Minority Rights Group International, 379 Brixton Road, London SW9 7DE
Tel: +44 (0) 20 7978 9498 Fax: +44 (0) 20 7738 6265
Email: minority.rights@mrgmail.org Website: www.minorityrights.org

Newham Conflict and Change Project

Runs excellent workshops for schools throughout the country on conflict resolution.

Newham Conflict and Change Project, Newham Conflict and Change, Christopher House, 2A Streatfield Avenue, East Ham, London E6 2LA
Tel: +44 (0) 20 8552 2050 Fax:+44 (0) 20 8470 5505
Email:conflict_change@btconnect.com
Website:www.conflictandchange.co.uk

Nonviolent Communication (NVC)

A process of communication developed by international peace-builder Marshall Rosenberg to enable people to communicate with respect, compassion and honesty. It leads to being heard and understood, communicating clearly without blame or judgement, and choosing actions that are in harmony with each others' needs and values. NVC offer a range of courses nationwide. For more information, contact:

Bridget Belgrave, Tel: +44 (0) 845 456 1050
Email: nvc@LifeResources.org.uk Website: www.LifeResources.org.uk

Nonviolent Direct Action in Britain

This site has been developed to provide cross-movement and online information about nonviolent direct actions taking place in Britain. It aims to offer regular events listings for anti-militarist, environmental and other activists working on a range of different issues. Nonviolent Direct Action also republish Britain's only cross-movement, monthly, nonviolent print-magazine, *Nonviolent Action*. They also offer useful texts and practical resources for nonviolent direct activists.

Website: www.nvda-uk.net

OneWorld

An online civil society network, supporting people's media to help build a more just global society. Offers comprehensive and professional production services to NGOs and charities to build a better world. Training and voluntary work possible all over the world.

OneWorld, 2nd Floor, River House, 143–145 Farringdon Road,
London EC1R 3AB
Tel: +44 (0) 20 7833 8347 Fax: +44 (0) 20 7833 3347
Email: justice@oneworld.net or foundation@oneworld.net
Website: www.oneworld.net

Oxford Research Group (ORG)

ORG combines rigorous research into nuclear weapons, arms control and conflict resolution with an understanding of the people who make those decisions. The areas of research also include the reduction and control of the arms trade, the 'war on terrorism' and the effective nonviolent resolution of conflict. ORG's work involves promoting accountability and transparency, providing information on current decisions so that public debate can take place, and fostering dialogue between those who disagree. ORG regularly brings policymakers — senior government officials, the military, strategists and scientists — together with independent experts to develop ways past the obstacles to nuclear disarmament, non-proliferation and greater global security. The aim is to build bridges of understanding as a means of opening up new ideas and to make possible significant new thinking on policy.

Oxford Research Group, 51 Plantation Road, Oxford OX2 6JE
Tel: +44 (0) 1865 242 819 Fax: +44 (0) 1865 794 652
Website: www.oxfordresearchgroup.org.uk

Peace Brigades International (PBI)

A non-governmental organization which protects human rights and promotes nonviolent transformation of conflicts. When invited, PBI sends teams of volunteers into areas of repression and conflict. The volunteers accompany human rights defenders, their organizations and others threatened by political violence. Perpetrators of human rights abuses usually do not want the world to witness their actions. The presence of volunteers backed by a support network helps to deter violence. This creates space for local activists to work for social justice and human rights.

Peace Brigades International, International Office, Unit 5,
89-93 Fonthill Rd, London N4 3HT
Tel: +44 (0) 20 7561 9141 Fax: +44 (0) 20 7281 3181
Email: info@peacebrigades.org Website: www.peacebrigades.org

Peace Centre for Warrington Children for Peace UK

A leading organization in the development of young people's peace-building skills which will help resolve 'conflict' nonviolently. They offer accredited educational programmes and activities, and need volunteers, gift-aid donations, commitment of regular giving (yearly, quarterly, monthly), and event/programme sponsorship.

The Peace Centre, Great Sankey, Peace Drive, Warrington WA5 1HQ
Tel: +44 (0) 1925 581 231 Fax: +44 (0) 1925 581 233
Email: info@childrenforpeace.org Website: www.childrenforpeace.org

Peace Exchange, Quakers

The Peace Exchange web pages are managed by Quaker Peace and Social Witness as a resource for everyone. It is possible to find information on events, campaigns and peace vigils. Pages change frequently at times of international crisis or for urgent action.

Website: www.peaceexchange.org.uk

Peace One Day

Peace One Day aims to raise global awareness of the annual United Nations International Day of Peace, a day of global ceasefire and nonviolence on 21 September. In this they engage civil society in the peaceful observance of a day of global unity. They influence governments, organizations within the United Nations, and regional and non-governmental organizations to initiate and support life-saving, educational, interfaith and public awareness activities.

Peace One Day, Block D, The Old Truman Brewery, 91 Brick Lane,
London E1 6QL
Tel: +44 (0) 20 7456 9180 Fax: +44 (0) 20 7375 2007
Email: info@peaceoneday.org Website: www.peaceoneday.org

Peaceworkers UK

Peaceworkers UK aim to contribute to the alleviation of suffering caused by violent conflict through the promotion and encouragement of civilian strategies for the prevention, management and resolution of conflict. They do this by developing and running training courses to prepare people for practical work in conflict areas, developing assessment standards for ensuring the quality of personnel working in this field, setting up a register of qualified personnel available in the UK, by promoting the establishment of a UK Civilian Peace Service and supporting similar international efforts in this field.

Peaceworkers UK, 18a Victoria Park Square, London E2 9PB
Tel: +44 (0) 20 8880 6070 Fax: +44 (0) 20 8880 6089
Email:info@peaceworkers.org.uk Website: www.peaceworkers.org.uk

Quaker Peace and Social Witness

The Quaker Peace and Social Witness works to create the conditions of peace and justice locally, nationally and internationally through a number of long-term work programmes. By placing workers in areas of current or recent conflict, the organization supports local capacities for building peace and social justice. Quaker representatives at the United Nations in Geneva facilitate dialogue between diplomats and non-governmental organizations on human rights, disarmament and international development issues. In Britain, Quakers engage with policymakers, raise public awareness, stimulate reflection and enable action for change on a range of peace and social issues.

Website: www.quaker.org.uk/peace

Responding to Conflict

Provide advice, cross-cultural training and longer-term support to people working for peace, development, rights and humanitarian assistance in societies affected or threatened by violent conflict.

Responding to Conflict, 1046 Bristol Road, Birmingham B29 6LJ
Tel: +44 (0) 121 415 5641 Fax/answerphone: +44 (0) 121 415 4119
Email: enquiries@respond.org Website: www.respond.org

The Richardson Institute for Peace Studies and Conflict Research

A research centre within the Department of Politics and International Relations at Lancaster University, which aims to promote a better understanding of the conditions of peaceful change and encourage practical application of its work.

The Richardson Institute for Peace and Conflict Research,
Department of Politics and International Relations,
Lancaster University, Lancaster LA1 4YL
Tel: +44 (0) 1524 594262 Fax: +44 (0) 1524 494238
Email: ri@lancaster.ac.uk Website: www.lancs.ac.uk

Rissho Kosei-kai (RKK)

RKK fund projects with the aim of restoring humanity to society through such social activities as blood donation and charitable fund-raising. Their firm belief is that people of religion the world over, as well as others whose activities are rooted in the spirit of religion, should cooperate in a way transcending sectarian differences to promote such activities from the broad-based viewpoint of social and public well-being.

Rissho Kosei-kai of the UK, c/o International Association for Religious Freedom, 2 Market Street, Oxford OX1 3EF
Tel: +44 (0) 1865 241 131 Fax: +44 (0) 1865 202 746
Email:rkk-uk@jais.co.uk Website:www.rk-world.org

Royal Institute for International Affairs (RIIA)

Also known as Chatham House, the RIIA is one of the world's leading institutes for the analysis of international issues. RIIA is membership-based and aims to help individuals and organizations to be at the forefront of developments in an ever-changing and increasingly complex world.

Royal Institute for International Affairs, Chatham House,
10 St James's Square, London SW1Y 4LE
Tel: +44 (0) 20 7957 5700 Fax: +44 (0) 20 7957 5710
Email: contact@riia.org Website: www.riia.org

Royal United Services Institute for Defence and Security Studies

Its purpose is to study, promote debate, report and provide options on all issues relating to national and international defence and security.

Royal United Services Institute, Whitehall, London SW1A 2ET
Tel: +44 (0) 20 7930 5854 Fax: +44 (0) 20 7321 0943
Email: information@rusi.org Website: www.rusi.org

Saferworld

Saferworld aims to spread information across borders, create a network of all environmentally interested people and above all encourage people to stand up for a healthier environment and a safer world.

Saferworld, 28 Charles Square, London N1 6HT
Tel: +44 (0) 20 7324 4646 Fax: +44 (0) 20 7324 4647
Email: info@safer-world.org Website: www.saferworld.org.uk

Scottish Centre for Nonviolence

The centre shares experience of using nonviolence at home, at work and in the community. It organizes nonviolence training and workshops, and also promotes training modules for universities and statutory bodies. Its library and resource materials are accessible to the public.

> The Scottish Centre for Nonviolence, The Annexe, Kirk Street,
> Dunblane, Scotland FK15 0AJ Tel: + 44 (0) 1786 824730
> Email: nonviolence@callnetuk.com
> Website: www.nonviolence-scotland.org.uk

Womankind Worldwide

Works internationally to raise the status of women, equipping them with the skills, knowledge and confidence to challenge discrimination and oppression and make positive changes in their own lives — for the benefit of all.

> Womankind Worldwide, 2nd Floor, 32–37 Cowper Street,
> London EC2A 4AW
> Tel: +44 (0) 20 7549 5700 Fax: +44 (0) 20 7549 5701
> Email: info@womankind.org.uk Website: www.womankind.org.uk

University Departments and Centres at:

Aberystwyth

The Aberystwyth Forum on Humanitarian Affairs was established by staff and postgraduate students in 1995 as an interdisciplinary discussion group to debate and explore issues on human rights and humanitarianism. The Forum aims to provide an informal setting for the growing number of people concerned with study and practice of human rights, humanitarianism and associated areas.

> University of Wales, Aberystwyth, Old College, King Street, Aberystwyth,
> Ceredigion SY23 2AX Tel: +44 (0) 1970 623111
> Email: bll7@aber.ac.uk Email: irm98@aber.ac.uk

Bradford
Centre for Conflict Resolution

The Centre is located within Bradford University's Peace Studies Department. From the beginning, emphasis has been placed on combining the ideas and experiences of both academics and practitioners and on the transference of research findings into practical applications.

Centre for Conflict Resolution, Department of Peace Studies,
University of Bradford, West Yorkshire BD7 1DP
Tel: +44 (0) 1274 235 235 Fax: +44 (0) 1274 235 240
Email: enquiries@bradford.ac.uk Website: www.brad.ac.uk/acad/peace

Cardiff
Department of International Relations

Department of International Relations,
Cardiff University, Cardiff CF10 3XQ
Tel: +44 (0) 29 2087 4000 Website: www.cardiff.ac.uk

Coventry
Centre for the Study of Forgiveness and Reconciliation

The Centre focuses on the study of nonviolent means of peace building and, in particular, the significance of processes of reconciliation and forgiveness in conflict transformation. On-going research projects at the Centre include comparative studies of how successor regimes deal with a legacy of violence and gross human rights abuse. Other research has concentrated on south and east Asian approaches to conflict transformation, peace building in Kosovo, and prospects for peaceful coexistence in the Middle East.

Centre for the Study of Forgiveness and Reconciliation,
Coventry University, Priory Street, Coventry CV1 5FB
Tel: +44 (0) 24 7688 7448
Email: a.rigby@coventry.ac.uk Website: www.coventry.ac.uk

Kent
The Centre for Conflict and Peace (CCP)

CCP is the successor to the long-established Centre for Conflict Analysis (CCA) founded in the 1960s. The practical activity of the CCA continues and includes a role in track-two mediation in protracted international conflicts around the world. Research interests of the CCP include international relations and international history, including international organization and conflict resolution; conflict analysis and resolution, mediation and intervention in Africa; European security and its institutions, and the legitimacy of security institutions in the post-cold war area; theories and methods of international relations, war and conflict studies, and conflict management with an emphasis on its institutional aspects; international relations, international organization and conflict studies.

The Centre for Conflict and Peace, The University of Kent,
Canterbury, Kent CT2 7NZ.
Tel: +44 (0) 1227 764 000
Email: T.K.Saalfeld@kent.ac.uk Website: www.kent.ac.uk

St Andrews
The Centre for the Study of Terrorism and Political Violence
The Centre aims to investigate the roots of political violence, to develop a body of theory spanning its various disparate elements, and to study the impact of violence and responses to it, at societal, governmental and international levels.

Centre for the Study of Terrorism and Political Violence,
University of St Andrews, St Andrews, Fife KY16 9AL
Tel: +44 (0) 1334 476161 Fax: +44 (0) 1334 462937
Email: cstpv@st-andrews.ac.uk Website: www.st-andrews.ac.uk

Organizations and Contacts
Around the World

African Centre for the Constructive Resolution of Disputes (ACCORD)
ACCORD is an international civil-society organization working throughout Africa to bring appropriate African solutions to the challenges posed by conflict on the continent. Recognized by the United Nations as a model for Africa, ACCORD's reputation continues to grow, and the knowledge and experience of the organization is often called on from as far afield as East Timor, Cyprus and Sao Paolo.

ACCORD Head Office, Private Bag X018, Umhlanga Rocks, 4320, South Africa
Tel: +27 31 502 3908 Fax: +27 31 502 4160
Email: info@accord.org.za

ACCORD Cape Town Office, PO Box 388, Kasselsvlei, 7533, South Africa
Tel: +27 21 975 0460/1/2 Fax: +27 21 975 0466
Email: hayley@accord.org.za Website: www.accord.org.za

The Arias Foundation for Peace and Human Progress, Costa Rica
The mission of the Foundation is to promote just and peaceful societies in Central America and other regions.

The Arias Foundation for Peace and Human Progress, Apartado 8-6410-1000, San José, Costa Rica
Tel: +506 224 1919 Fax: +506 224 4949
Website: www.arias.or.cr

Association for Conflict Resolution, USA
Family mediation and training. Dedicated to enhancing the practice and public understanding of conflict resolution.

Association for Conflict Resolution, 1015 18th Street, NW, Suite 1150, Washington, DC 20036, USA
Tel: +1 (0) 202 464 9700 Fax: +1 (0) 202 464 9720
Email: acr@acresolution.org Website: www.acresolution.org

Canadian International Institute of Applied Negotiation (CIIAN), Canada

The CIIAN is dedicated to the prevention and resolution of destructive conflict at the local, national and international levels. CIIAN believes that conflict competency is a cornerstone for such achievement.

CIIAN, 280 Albert Street, Suite 201, Ottawa, Ontario, Canada K1P 5G8
Tel: +1 613 237 9050 Fax: +1 613 237 6952
Email: ciian@ciian.org
Website: www.ciian.org or http://www.canadr.com/home.htm

Canadian Peacebuilding Coordination Committee (CPCC), Canada

The Canadian Peacebuilding Coordinating Committee (CPCC) is a network of Canadian non-governmental organizations and institutions, academics and other individuals from a wide range of sectors, including humanitarian assistance, development, conflict resolution, peace, faith communities, and human rights. CPCC has been working to formulate policy and operational directions for Canadian NGOs involved in peace building, in collaboration with other relevant actors. The network is engaged in a process of dialogue with departments and agencies of the Government of Canada and a broad range of NGOs to articulate Canadian directions in the area of peace building, and to strengthen NGO and civil society input into peace-building policy and programme development.

Canadian Peacebuilding Coordinating Committee, 1 Nicholas Street, #1216, Ottawa, Ontario, K1N 7B7, Canada
Tel: +1 613 241 3446 Fax: + 613 241 4846
Email: chris@peacebuild.ca Website: www.peacebuild.ca

The Center for Conflict Resolution, Salisbury University, USA

The goal of the Center is to study, examine and address the nature of conflict and to teach, promote and foster nonviolent, collaborative and peaceful ways to resolve such conflicts. They offer training for practitioners of conflict resolution.

The Center for Conflict Resolution, Salisbury University,
1100 Camden Avenue, Salisbury, Md 21801, USA
Tel: +1 (0) 410 219 2873 Fax: +1 (0) 410 219 2879
Email: conflictresolution@salisbury.edu Website: www.salisbury.edu

Centre for Conflict Resolution, South Africa

The Centre for Conflict Resolution seeks to contribute towards a just peace in Africa by promoting constructive, creative and cooperative approaches to the resolution of conflict and the reduction of violence. Mediation, facilitation, training, education and research comprise the Centre's main activities, with an emphasis on capacity building.

Centre for Conflict Resolution, University of Cape Town,
Rhodes Gift Post Office, 7707 South Africa
Tel: +27 21 4222512 Fax: +27 21 4222622
Email: mailbox@ccr.uct.ac.za Website: http://ccrweb.ccr.uct.ac.za

Center for Conflict Resolution (CECORE), Uganda

The Center for Conflict Resolution is an initiative of Ugandan people working to seek alternative and creative means of preventing, managing and resolving conflicts. Members come from a rich background of peace and human rights work, research and training. CECORE is a non-profit, non-governmental organization with programmes in the Great Lakes Region and the Greater Horn of Africa Region, the rest of Africa and in the Asia/Pacific region.

Center for Conflict Resolution, Uganda, c/o CECORE, Pilkington Road,
NIC Building, 6th Floor, PO Box 5211, Kampala, Uganda
Tel: +256 41 341 069, +256 41 255 033 Fax: +256 41 255 033
Email: cecore@swiftuganda.com Email: uganda@coexistence.net
Website: www.coexistence.net

Centre for Dialogue and Reconciliation, India

With its main focus on dialogue between the different castes, religions and genders of India and Pakistan, the Centre for Dialogue and Reconciliation (CDR) wants to serve as a catalyst for peace and reconciliation. This non-profit, non-governmental organization holds conferences and discussions. The Centre initiates independent research and forms action plans for the conflict areas in the region. The main conflict prevention programme, Dialogues of Understanding, deals with the conflict in Kashmir and Jammu. It aims to build deeper trust amongst all sections of Kashmiri society.

Centre for Dialogue and Reconciliation, J-1346 Palam Vihar, Gurgaon,
Haryana 122 017, India
Tel: +91 124 646 0602
Email: sushobha@vsnl.com or cdrec@vsnl.in

Centre Medical Evangelique, Kenya

The Evangelical Medical Centre serves an immediate population of around
156,000, and facilitates medical services in an area the size of France and with
a population of around 8,000,000.

The Centre has four goals:

1. to preach the gospel of Jesus Christ;
2. to train medical and paramedical workers for the service of the church;
3. to serve other centres as a referral hospital with specialist doctors and
   specialist care;
4. to serve as a distribution centre for medicines and medical supplies to
   other centres.

Centre Medical Evangelique, Nyankunde, République Démocratique
du Congo, P.O. Box 21285, Nairobi, Kenya
Tel: +871 761231279 Fax: +871 761231280
Email: cmenyan@cmenyan.uuplus.com Website: www.nyankunde.org

Centre Résolution Conflits (CRC)

CRC in Nyankunde-Bunia (Democratic Republic of Congo) is a multi-faith
non-governmental organization with a local, national, regional and international presence. It is a forum whose base components are made up of peace
committees in villages, churches, mosques, universities and higher institutions,
and which share a common spirit in peace and conflict resolution matters.

Kenya

Mrs Kongosi Mussanzi, Centre Résolution Conflits,
Nyankunde-Bunia (DRC), PO Box 21285 Nairobi, Kenya
Email: crc@cmenyan.uuplus.com

UK

Ben Mussanzi wa Mussangu, 43 Rothersay Terrace, University of Bradford,
Bradford BD7 1QE, UK
Email: Mussanzi@yahoo.co.uk
Website: http://crc-congo.tripod.com/index-_E.html

The Coexistence Initiative, USA

The Coexistence Initiative seeks to catalyse a global awareness of and commitment to the creation of a world accepting of difference. It works to encourage a positive and proactive embrace of diversity. TCI sees the goal of this proactive embrace of diversity as ensuring freedom from fear of discrimination on grounds of identity while simultaneously encouraging robust civic policies. In pursuit of its goals, TCI works with grass-roots communities, practitioners in a wide variety of fields, and policy-makers at the local, national and international levels.

The Coexistence Initiative USA, 477 Madison Avenue, Fourth Floor, New York, NY 10022, USA
Tel: 1+ (0) 212 303 9445 Fax: +1 (0) 212 980 4027
Email: info@coexistence.net

Conflict Resolution Center International, USA

A non-profit organization promoting nonviolent conflict resolution. Home of one of the largest libraries on conflict and dispute resolution.

Conflict Resolution Center International, Inc., 204 Thirty-seventh Street, Pittsburgh, PA 15201-1859, USA
Tel: +1 (0) 412 687 6210 Fax: +1 (0) 412 687 6232
Email: Paul@ConflictRes.org Website: www.conflictres.org

Conflict Resolution Network, Australia

Their vision is to create conflict-resolving community in a culture of peace and social justice. Conflict Resolution builds stronger and more cohesive organizations and more rewarding relationships, so they make CR skills, strategies and attitudes more readily and universally accessible.

The Conflict Resolution Network, PO Box 1016, Chatswood, Australia NSW 2057
Tel: +61 (0) 2 9419 8500 Fax: +61 (0) 2 9413 1148
Email: crn@crnhq.org Website: www.crnhq.org

Disarmament and Security Centre, New Zealand

Promoting secure alternatives to nuclear weapons.

Disarmament and Security Centre, PO Box 8390, 35 Rata Street,
Riccarton, Christchurch, Aotearoa/New Zealand
Tel: +64 3 348 1353, +64 3 348 1350 Fax: +64 3 348 1353
Email: robwcpuk@chch.planet.org.nz or kate@chch.planet.org.nz
Website: www.disarmsecure.org

European Platform for Conflict Prevention and Transformation

An open network of some 150 key European organizations working in the field
of the prevention and/or resolution of violent conflicts in the international
arena. Its mission is to facilitate the exchange of information and experience
among participating organizations, as well as to stimulate cooperation and
synergy. It is an independent non-governmental organization based in the
Netherlands. Its mission is to contribute to prevention and resolution of
violent conflicts in the world.

The European Centre for Conflict Prevention,
PO Box 14069, 3508 SC Utrecht, The Netherlands
Tel: +31 (0) 30 242 7777 Fax: + 31 (0) 30 236 9268
Email: info@conflict-prevention.net

Visiting address:
Korte Elisabethstraat 6, 3511 JG Utrecht, The Netherlands

Postal address:
PO Box 14069, 3508 SC Utrecht, The Netherlands,
Website: www.euconflict.org

The Fellowship of Reconciliation, USA

The Fellowship envisions a world of justice, peace and freedom. It is a revolutionary vision of a beloved community where differences are respected, conflicts addressed nonviolently, oppressive structures dismantled, and where people live in harmony with the earth, nurtured by diverse spiritual traditions that foster compassion, solidarity and reconciliation. They educate, train, build coalitions, and engage in nonviolent and compassionate actions locally, nationally and globally.

The Fellowship of Reconciliation, Box 271, Nyack, NY 10960, USA
Tel: +1 (0) 845 358 4601 Fax: +1 (0) 845 358 4924
Email: for@forusa.org Website: www.forusa.org

Gandhi Peace Foundation, India

The Gandhi Peace Foundation was established to study and promote the relevance of the nonviolent alternative bequeathed by Mahatma Gandhi with respect to present-day problems. It publishes books linking Gandhian ideals to different areas such as economics, pollution, disarmament and social conflicts. Promotion also takes place by means of fellowships, youth camps, training programmes in nonviolence and social change, and the international network with individuals and Gandhian groups. The Foundation has stimulated peace initiatives in Nagaland, Assam, Punjab and Kashmir, and has intervened in the deeper causes of disturbances in some regions through relief and rehabilitation measures.

Gandhi Peace Foundation, 221–223, Deen Dayal Upadhyama Marg, New Delhi 110 002, India
Tel: +91 11 323 7491/ 323 7493 Fax: +91 11 323 6734
Email: avard@del3.vsnl.net.in

Hague Appeal for Peace

The Hague Appeal for Peace is an international network of peace and justice organizations dedicated to sowing the seeds for the abolition of war through the implementation of the Hague Agenda for Peace and Justice for the 21st Century (UN Ref A/54/98). This agenda is a set of 50 recommendations developed at the Hague Appeal for Peace Conference in 1999, the largest inter-national peace conference in history. They are focused on promoting a global campaign for peace education dedicated to the integration of peace education into curricula and communities worldwide as a means of reducing violence and preventing war.

Geneva Office
c/o IPB, 41 Rue de Zurich, CH-1201 Geneva Switzerland
Tel: +41 22 731 6429 Fax: +41 22 738 9419
Email: hap@ipb.org

New York Office
c/o IWTC, 777 UN Plaza, New York, NY 10017 USA
Tel: +1 (0) 212 687 2623 Fax: +1 (0) 212 661 2704
Email: hap@haguepeace.org Website: www.haguepeace.org

Human Rights Watch

Human Rights Watch is an independent, non-governmental organization dedicated to protecting the human rights of people worldwide. They have offices all around the world:

USA

New York
350 Fifth Avenue, 34th floor, New York, NY 10118-3299, USA
Tel: +1 212 290 4700 Fax: +1 212 736 1300
Email: hrwnyc@hrw.org

Washington, DC
1630 Connecticut Avenue, N.W., Suite 500, Washington, DC 20009, USA
Tel: +1 202 612 4321 Fax: +1 202 612 4333
Email: hrwdc@hrw.org

Los Angeles
11500 W. Olympic Blvd., Suite 441, Los Angeles, CA 90064, USA
Tel: +1 310 477 5540 Fax: +1 310 477 4622
Email: hrwla@hrw.org

San Francisco
312 Sutter Street, Suite 407, San Francisco CA 94108, USA
Tel: +1 415 362 3250 Fax: +1 415 362 3255
Email: hrwsf@hrw.org

United Kingdom
2nd Floor, 2–12 Pentonville Road, London N1 9HF, UK
Tel: +44 (0) 20 7713 1995 Fax: +44 (0) 20 7713 1800
Email: hrwuk@hrw.org

Belgium
Rue Van Campenhout 15, 1000 Brussels, Belgium
Tel: +32 2 732-2009 Fax: +32 2 732-0471
Email: hrwatcheu@skynet.be

Switzerland
8 rue des Vieux-Grenadiers, 1205 Geneva, Switzerland,
Tel: +41 22 320 55 90 Fax: +41 22 320 55 11
E-mail: hrwgva@hrw.org Website: www.hrw.org

Independent Human Rights Commission, Afghanistan

The Afghan Independent Human Rights Commission, established in June 2002, is based on the provision of the Bonn agreement. The mandate for the AIHRC is to support and facilitate the development of a sustainable independent national capacity for the promotion and protection of human rights in Afghanistan.

Email: help@aihrc.org.af Website: www.aihrc.org.af/000.html

Indian Confederation of Indigenous and Tribal Peoples North East Zone (ICITP-NEZ), India

Focused on peace and all-round sustainable development of the indigenous and tribal peoples in north-east India. Areas of activity are culture, environment, education, peace, poverty, gender, health and human rights.

ICITP-NEZ, St John's Mission, Bijni, PO Bijni, Bongaigaon, Assam, India
Tel: +91 3664 84004 Fax: +91 3664 84004
Email: jebrabodo@rediffmail.com

Institute for Conflict Management, India

The Institute for Conflict Management (ICM) is an autonomous, non-governmental, non-profit society engaged in the search for solutions to the widening sphere of conflict and violence in south Asia. The Institute's primary concerns are collective violence, which threatens the fabric of civil society in the modern states, in particular, terrorism and internal security. ICM collaborates intensively with governmental agencies, academic institutions and grass-roots voluntary organizations. Target groups range from international and national policy-makers to civil institutions and populations in south-east Asia.

Institute for Conflict Management, 11, Talkatora Road,
New Delhi 110 001, India
Tel: +91 11 371 5455/0374/0375 Fax: +91 11 373 6471
Email: icm@del3.vsnl.net.in Website: www.satp.org

The Institute for International Mediation and Conflict Resolution (IIMCR), USA

A Washington, DC based, non-profit institution whose mission is to promote the use of peaceful conflict resolution techniques among a generation of future leaders through the design and implementation of unique programmes and services.

The Institute for International Mediation and Conflict Resolution
1424 K Street, NW, Suite 650, Washington, DC 20005, USA
Tel: +1 (0) 202 347 2042 Fax: +1 (0) 202 347 2440
Email: info@iimcr.org Website: www.iimcr.org

Institute of Peace and Conflict Studies (IPCS), India

Established as an independent think-tank devoted to studying security issues relating to South Asia, leading strategic thinkers, academicians, former members of the civil services, foreign services, armed forces, police forces, paramilitary forces and media persons (print and electronic) have been associated with the Institute in its endeavour to chalk out a comprehensive framework for security studies — one that can cater to the changing demands of national, regional and global security.

Institute of Peace and Conflict Studies
246 Vasant Enclave, New Delhi 110057, India
Tel: +91 11 26153160, +91 11 26152743, +91 11 26146285,
+91 11 26146478, +91 11 26149087 Tel/Fax: +91 11 26152009
Email: officemail@ipcs.org Website: www.ipcs.org

International Centre for Peace Initiatives (ICPI), India

Established in Mumbai, India to conceptualize, develop and promote innovative approaches to peace at global, regional and national levels. It acts as a catalyst in partnership with like-minded institutions. It sees its role as a social entrepreneur at the leading edge of the south Asian public policy agenda.

Website: http://strategicforesight.com/ICPI

The International Conflict Resolution Centre, University of Melbourne, Australia

The International Conflict Resolution Centre is a thriving, interdisciplinary learning community committed to the development of cultures of peace.

The International Conflict Resolution Centre,
The University of Melbourne, Victoria 3010, Australia
Tel: +61 (0) 3 8344 7035 Fax: +61 (0) 3 9347 6618
Email: icrc@psych.unimelb.edu.au
Website: http://www.psych.unimelb.edu.au/icrc

International Crisis Group (ICG), USA

An independent, non-profit, multinational organization, with over 90 staff members on five continents, working through field-based analysis and high-level advocacy to prevent and resolve deadly conflict.

ICG, 420 Lexington Avenue, Suite 2640, New York 10170, USA
Tel: +1 (0) 202 785 1601 Fax: +1 (0) 202 785 1630
Email: icgny@crisisweb.org Website: www.crisisweb.org

Committee of the International Red Cross

Website: www.icrc.org

Israeli Centre for Human Rights in the Occupied Territories B'Tselem, Israel

Established by a group of prominent academics, attorneys, journalists and Knesset members. It endeavours to document and educate the Israeli public and policy-makers about human rights violations in the Occupied Territories, combat the phenomenon of denial prevalent among the Israeli public, and help create a human rights culture in Israel.

Email: mail@btselem.org Website: www.btselem.org

The International Federation of Red Cross and Red Crescent Societies

Website: www.ifrc.org

Israel/Palestine Centre for Research and Information (IPCRI), Israel

IPCRI, founded in Jerusalem in 1988, is the only joint Israeli-Palestinian public policy think-tank in the world. It is devoted to developing practical solutions to the Israeli-Palestinian conflict.

IPCRI, PO Box 9321, Jerusalem 91092, Israel
Tel: +972 2 676 9460 Fax: +972 2 676 8011
Website: www.ipcri.org and www.place4peace.com

Other programmes:
Joint Environmental Mediations Programme: www.ipcri.org/jems
Our Shared Environment: www.our-shared-environment.net

Murder Victims' Families for Reconciliation, USA

Founded in 1976, Murder Victims' Families for Reconciliation is a national
organization of family members of both homicide and state killings who oppose
the death penalty in all cases. This mission is to abolish the death penalty.
They advocate for programmes and policies that reduce the rate of homicide
and promote crime prevention and alternatives to violence. They support programmes that address the needs of victims, helping them to rebuild their lives.

Murder Victims' Families for Reconciliation
2161 Massachusetts Avenue, Cambridge, MA 02140, USA
Tel: +1 617 868 0007 Fax: +1 617 354 2832
Email: info@mvfr.org Website: www.mvfr.org

Niwano Peace Foundation, Japan

The Niwano Peace Foundation was chartered in 1978 to contribute to the
realization of world peace and the enhancement of culture by promoting
research and other activities, based on a religious spirit and serving the cause
of peace in such fields as thought, culture, science and education.

Niwano Peace Foundation, Shamvilla Catherina 5F, 1-16-9 Shinjuku,
Shinjuku-ku, Tokyo, 160 0022 Japan
Tel: +3 (0) 3226 4371 Fax: +3 (0) 3226 1835
Email: info@npf.or.jp Website: www.npf.or.jp

Nonviolent Peaceforce

Their mission is to facilitate the creation of a trained, international civilian
peace-force committed to third-party nonviolent intervention. At the invi-
tation of local groups, Peaceforce will deploy hundreds of peace-workers to
protect human rights, prevent violence, and enable peaceful resolution of
conflict. Peaceforce uses proven methodologies and has been endorsed by
world and local leaders in peace and conflict resolution, including seven Nobel
Peace Laureates.

USA:
Nonviolent Peaceforce, 801 Front Avenue, St Paul, MN 55103, USA

Canada:
Nonviolent Peaceforce Canada, 211 Bronson Avenue #309A,
Ottawa, Ontario K1R 6H5, Canada

Other:
Nonviolent Peaceforce, Rue Van Elewyck 35, 1050 Bruxelles, Belgium
Email: info@nonviolentpeaceforce.org
Website: www.nonviolentpeaceforce.org

Palestinian Center for Peace and Democracy (PCPD), Israel

A non-profit, non-governmental Palestinian organization dedicated to promoting concepts of democracy, peace, social justice, human rights and civic education in the Palestinian areas. Founded in 1992 by a group of Palestinian intellectuals and professionals to create a forum for free and uncensored dialogue, the PCPD mobilizes support for a comprehensive and lasting peace in the Middle East.

Palestinian Center for Peace and Democracy
Ramallah — al-Sahel Street, PO Box 2290 Ramallah, Israel
Tel: +970 2 2965981/2 Fax: +970 2 2965983
Email: pcpd@palnet.com Website: www.pcpd.org

Pax Christi International

Pax Christi International is a non-profit, non-governmental Catholic peace movement working on a global scale on a wide variety of issues in the fields of human rights, security and disarmament, economic justice and ecology. They have offices all over the world. For general information, please contact:

Pax Christi International,
Rue du Vieux Marche aux Grains 21, 1000 Brussels, Belgium
Tel: +32 2 5025550 Fax: +32 2 502.46.26
Email: hello@paxchristi.net Website: www.paxchristi.net

Peace Now (Shalom Achshav), Israel

Shalom Achshav, the largest grass-roots movement in Israel's history, was founded in March 1978 by 348 reserve commanders, officers, and combat soldiers of the Israel defence forces. Experience had taught these citizen soldiers that only a politically negotiated solution could end their nation's hundred-year war with its Arab and Palestinian neighbours. Since its inception, it has been instrumental in advancing political solutions to the discord between Israelis and Arabs. Shalom Achshav believes a secure peace can best be achieved through Israeli withdrawal to safe borders from the West Bank and Gaza; creation of a Palestinian state subject to strict military limitations; negotiation of security and peace accords between Israel and Syria leading to a safe Israeli withdrawal from the Golan Heights; and a resolution on the status of an undivided Jerusalem that accomodates the national aspirations and religious needs of both Israeli and Palestinian residents.

Email: info@peacenow.org.il Website: http://www.peacenow.org.il

Americans for Peace Now (APN) National Headquarters
1101 14th Street, NW, 6th Floor, Washington, DC 20005, USA
Tel: +1 202 728 1893 Fax: +1 202 728 1895
Email: apndc@peacenow.org

New York Office
114 West 26th Street, Suite 1000, New York, NY 10001, USA

Los Angeles Office
5870 West Olympic Blvd. Los Angeles, CA 90036, USA
Tel: +1 323 934 3480 Fax: +1 323 934 3550
Email: apnwest@netzero.net Website: www.peacenow.org

Pioneers of Change and Common Futures

Pioneers of Change is an emerging global learning community of committed young people in their 20s and early 30s, from diverse cultural, social and professional backgrounds. Together they set up and run community projects around the world.

Pioneers of Change,
PO Box 197, Westhoven 2142, Johannesburg, South Africa
Phone/Fax : +27 (11) 624 3704

Pioneers of Change,
c/o Thygesen, Snorresgade 8, 5. tv., 2300 Copenhagen S, Denmark
Email: mille@pioneersofchange.net
Website: www.pioneersofchange.net

Search For Common Ground, USA

Committed to building models showing that even the most difficult problems can be resolved peacefully.

Search For Common Ground, 1601 Connecticut Avenue, NW, Suite 200, Washington, DC 20009-1035, USA
Tel: +1 (0) 202 265 4300 Fax: +1 (0) 202 232 6718
Email: search@sfc.org Website: www.sfc.org

Seeds of Peace, USA

Empowering children of war to break the cycle of violence. A non-profit, non-political organization dedicated to preparing teenagers from areas of conflict to develop the leadership skills required to promote coexistence and peace. Focuses primarily on the Middle East, though its programmes have expanded to include other areas of conflict. Seeds of Peace International Summer Camp helps to bring together Arab and Israeli, Turkish and Cypriot, Indian and Pakistani, and many teenagers from warring countries before fear, mistrust and prejudice blind them from seeing the human face of their enemy.

Seeds of Peace,
370 Lexington Avenue, Suite 401, New York, NY 10017, USA
Tel: +1 (0) 212 573 8404 Fax: +1 (0) 212 573 8047
Email: info@seedsofpeace.org
Email for Summer Camp: camp@seedsofpeace.org
Website: www.seedsofpeace.org

September Eleventh Families for Peaceful Tomorrows, USA

Peaceful Tomorrows is an advocacy organization founded by family members of September 11 victims who have united to turn grief into action for peace. Their mission is to seek effective, nonviolent solutions to terrorism, and to acknowledge a common experience with all people similarly affected by violence throughout the world. By conscientiously exploring peaceful options in the search for justice, they hope to spare additional families the suffering they have experienced — as well as to break the cycle of violence and retaliation engendered by war. In doing so, they work to create a safer world for the present and future generations.

September Eleventh Families for Peaceful Tomorrows
P.O. Box 1818, Peter Stuyvesant Station, New York, NY 10009, USA
Tel: +1 (646) 408 5676 Email: Colleen@peacefultomorrows.org
Website: www.peacefultomorrows.org

Shuhada Organization, Afghanistan

A non-governmental and non-profit organization committed to the reconstruction and development of Afghanistan with special emphasis on the empowerment of women and children.

Shuhada Organization
c/o Shuhada Clinic, Alamdar Road, Naseer Abad, Quetta, Pakistan
Fax: +92 1 630 214 3097
Email: info@shuhada.org Website: www.shuhada.org

UNESCO (United Nations Educational, Scientific and Cultural Organization)

Website: www.unesco.org

University of Florida, USA

Conflict Resolution/Peer Mediation Research Project. Offering workshops on conflict resolution skills, and managing anger and aggression in classrooms.

Email: conflict@coe.ufl.edu Website: www.ufl.edu

UNICEF (United Nations Children's Fund)

Website: www.unicef.org

UNOCHA (United Nations Office for the Coordination of Humanitarian Affairs)

Website: www.un.org.mk/ocha

Voices in the Wilderness, USA

Since its founding in 1996, Voices in the Wilderness has campaigned to end economic and military warfare against the Iraqi people. They have done this mostly by organizing delegations to Iraq in deliberate violation of UN economic sanctions and US law, to publicly deliver small amounts of medical supplies to children and families in need. Their primary focus has always been ordinary Iraqi civilians and the most vulnerable of Iraqi society, especially children. They have witnessed this ongoing warfare through the everyday lives of families they have come to know as friends over the course of 70 visits to Iraq.

Voices in the Wilderness
5315 N Clark Street, Box 634, Chicago, IL 60640, USA
Tel: +1 773 784 8065 Fax: +1 773 784 8837
Email: info@vitw.org Website: www.vitw.org

Witness, USA

A picture is worth a thousand words. Witness works with partners across the world to use video to overcome political, economic and physical barriers and expose human rights abuses.

Witness
333 Broadway, New York, NY 10013, USA
Tel: +1 212 274 1664 ext. 201 Fax: +1 212 274 1262
Email: witness@witness.org Website: www.witness.org

Directories and Further Links

Links to conflict resolution websites

www.geocities.com/Athens/8945/links.html

Conflict Resolution Resources

http://isca.indiana.edu/conflict.html

Development Issues Knowledge Centre: Peace and Conflict

www.dev-zone.org/knowledge/Peace_and_Conflict/
Conflict_Resolution/Organisations

People for Peace is an informational website listing many peace sites.

http://members.aol.com/pforpeace

University of Bradford: 'Guide to Conflict Resolution Organizations
in the UK' (page under construction)

www.bradford.ac.uk/acad/confres/crorgs/

CAIN Project

http://cain.ulst.ac.uk/

Conflict Prevention Network, CP-Net

http://www.conflict-prevention.org/

**Key Contacts of the European Platform for Conflict Prevention
and Transformation**

http://www.euconflict.org/dev/ECCP/ECCPSurveys_v0_10.nsf/vwILk
upWeb/KeyContacts?OpenDocument&Click=

Recommended Reading

Conflict resolution

Ackerman, P., and Duvall, J., *A Force More Powerful. A Century of Nonviolent Conflict,* New York: Palgrave, 2000
The authors describe how popular movements have used nonviolence to overthrow dictators, obstruct military invaders, and secure human rights in country after country over the past century.

Francis, D., *People, Peace and Power. Conflict Transformation in Action,* London: Pluto Press, 2002
This book looks at the role that ordinary people can play as peace builders in societies where violence and antagonism have become the norm, where intercommunal relationships are fractured or where institutions and the rule of law have collapsed. It examines theory and practice of conflict transformation and its relevance for different cultures and contexts.

European Platform for Conflict Prevention and Transformation, *People Building Peace,* Utrecht: European Platform for Conflict Prevention and Transformation, 1999
These are the stories of 35 people involved in peace building around the world.

European Platform for Conflict Prevention and Transformation, Searching for Peace in Africa, *An Overview of Conflict Prevention and Management Activities,* Utrecht: European Platform for Conflict Prevention and Transformation, 1999
This is a survey of conflict prevention and management activities in Africa. It provides background information, details of peace building, assessments of possible future developments, recommendations on how to solve conflicts and other information.

Lederach, J.P., *Building Peace: Sustainable Reconciliation in Divided Societies,* Washington DC: United States Institute of Peace, 1997
In this book Lederach illustrates his comprehensive framework for building peace and bringing reconciliation. It draws from the author's experience of working with individuals in violent conflict areas.

Miall, H., Ramsbotham, O., and Woodhouse, T., **Contemporary Conflict Resolution,** Cambridge: Polity Press, 1999
This is an insightful review of the early development of the field of conflict resolution which brings a much needed perspective on the challenges presented by late twentieth-century conflicts.

Nagler, M.N., **Is There No Other Way? The Search for a Nonviolent Future,** Berkeley CA: Berkeley Hills Books, 2001
The author shows how nonviolence can be the strategy for those who are looking for better ways than carnage for dealing with problems. Beginning with the achievements of Mahatma Gandhi, and following the legacy of nonviolence through a century of political, social and economic conflict, the book illustrates how nonviolence has proven its power against arms and injustice wherever it has been correctly understood and applied.

Wallensteen, P., **Understanding Conflict Resolution: War, Peace and the Global System,** London: Sage, 2002
This is a comprehensive book that covers conflict resolution and its application in wars between states, civil wars and conflicts of state formation. It also looks at regional conflicts and the role of the United Nations and the international community.

Training and skills

ACTION for Conflict Transformation, **Transforming Conflict. Reflections of Practitioners Worldwide,** Melville, South Africa: ACTION for Conflict Transformation, 2003
Addressed to those working on conflict transformation and peace building, this book is a collection of real-life examples and experiences from which the reader can gain insights about what might be possible or appropriate in a particular context.

Crum, T.M., **The Magic of Conflict. Turning a Life of Work into a Work of Art,** New York: Touchstone, 1981
This book illustrates a set of simple techniques (including meditation, breathing exercises, openness and play) that can help you move towards inner peace. Crum's approach will help you master conflicts and turn frustration into fulfilment. From overcoming apathy to understanding how conflict can be an opportunity for choice and change, this book turns mind-body integration principles into powerful tools.

Fisher, S., Ludin, J., Williams, S., Adbi, D.I., Smith, R., and Williams, S., *Working with Conflict. Skills and Strategies for Action,* London: Zed Books, 2000
Easy to use and well laid out, this book is addressed to those working in zones affected by violence. It includes helpful visual materials and provides a range of practical tools (processes, ideas, visual aids and techniques) for tackling conflict.

McConnell, C., *Change Activist. Make Big Things Happen Fast,* London: Pearson Education, 2001
An interesting book based on activist and corporate experience, it illustrates activist thinking and how it can be applied to one's career. The slogan goes: 'It's time to take control of your life. Be what makes the difference and change the world you work in. The only way to do it … is to do it.'

Rosenberg, M.B., *Nonviolent Communication: a Language of Life,* 2nd Ed., Eninitas CA: PuddleDancer Press, 2003
This book aims at helping the reader resolve conflict and develop relationships based on mutual respect, compassion and cooperation. It shows us how to reach beneath the surface and how all our actions are based on human needs, which we are seeking to meet. When we understand and acknowledge our needs, we create a shared basis for a more satisfying relationship — a deeper connection with others and ourselves.

Costs of conflict

Brown, M.E., and Rosencrance, R.N. (eds.), *The Costs of Conflict. Prevention and Cure in the Global Arena,* Lanham MD: Rowan and Littlefield, 1999
The authors look at the the true costs of conflict by examining a number of case studies and contribute considerably to the debate on conflict prevention by focusing on costs and benefits.